LITTLE THINGS THAT STICK IN THE *Mind*

Some Stories from My Life Experiences

ALLAN KROSCH

Little Things That Stick In The Mind –
Some Stories From My Life Experiences
Author: Allan Krosch
Brisbane Australia

Copyright © 2021 Allan Krosch
ISBN: 9780645062007
Subject: Memoir

Book production: www.bevryanpublish.com
Contact the author via www.bevryanpublish.com

 A catalogue record for this book is available from the National Library of Australia

All rights reserved. Except as permitted under the Australian Copyright Act 1968, no part of this publication may be reproduced, stored in a retrieval system, or transmitted in any form or by any means, electronic, mechanical, photocopying, recording or otherwise, without prior written permission. All enquiries should be made to the author.

Contents

Introduction 9

Chapter 1: Getting Started 11
    Great Motivators of Men 11
        Another Point of View *13*
    My German Connections 14
        Some Germanic DNA. *16*
        More on German Characteristics *17*
        Story of a German Character *17*
        An Aryan Connection? *19*
    Footnote About Cambridge University. 21

Chapter 2: Riposte; and My Linkage to Phoenicians
    (Through Marriage) 23
    Story from Our Wedding Reception 23
    Story About Riposte. 24
    The Only Real Wealth in Life. 25
    Story About My Ability to Sell. 26
    Stories About Jeha 27

Story About Purchasing a Dress for My Fiancée . . . 29
Story About Food Flavours 30

Chapter 3: Experiences from the United States
           and Europe 33
Stories from My Time at Purdue 33
Stories from Travel in Europe in 1972 34
    Story from Versailles *35*
    Story from Norway *35*
    Driving in Germany *36*
    Driving to Prague *38*
    Story from Madrid *40*

Chapter 4: Memories of Fishing and Tennis 43
Fishing at Clairview 43
Cooking Mud Crabs at Clairview 46
Memories of Tennis 47

Chapter 5: Singing and Joke Telling 49
Becoming a Member of the Brisbane Club 49
Story About Gentlemen's Clubs in Brisbane 51
Memories of Prince Philip 52
Music of the Century 53
Piano Story 55
Story of Hymn Singing 59
More on Music 60

  The Physics of Music. *60*
  A Memory for Lyrics. *61*
 Story About Telling Jokes on the Radio 63

Chapter 6: Memories 65
 Memories from Skiing 65
  Skiing in Colorado *66*
  Reflections on Skiing. *67*
 Jim Simpson – a New South Wales Patriot. 67
 Story from Expo 86 68
 My Female Neighbour's View About Women's Brains . 70
 My Experience on Sentry Duty in Oaklands Parade . 71
 Memories of *Cloud Street* 73
 Memories from My Time at Cribb Island State School 74

Chapter 7: More Stories 77
 Stories About Golf 77
  Advice Ignored *78*
  My Golf Routine *78*
  The Most Important Shots in Golf *79*
  Flukes at Golf *79*
  Par-3 Challenges *80*
  Consistency *81*
  Golf at the Royal Morocco Course in Marrakesh . . *81*
  Learnings from Golf *82*
  My Missed Career Opportunity. *83*

  More-Forgiving Roadsides *83*
 Story from the Moscow to St Petersburg Cruise . . . 84
  Another Story from the Russian Cruise. *85*
  A Further Story from the Russian Cruise *86*
 British Inventiveness 87
  How Times Change *87*
 Sleepwalking in Germany 88
 Story of an Ungiven Speech 93
 Another Story About Anniversaries 94
 Centenary of 26 Ascot Street 95
 Story About Doughnut Making at the
 Ascot School Fete 97
 Guarding Paintings in the Ascot School Hall. . . . 99

Chapter 8: Human Nature 101
 Story of My Speech to a Group of Young Engineers . 101
  It's Funny How Life Turns Out *102*
  The Webs That Interconnect People. *103*
  Little Things Can Have a Big Effect *104*
 Story from Nevada, USA 106
 Humans Are Creatures of Habit 108
 Human Affairs and Their Complexity 109
 Thoughts While Circling Over Sydney in an Aeroplane 110
 A Thought Whilst on the Roof of a Block of Units . . 111
 Optimising Efficiency of Supermarket Shopping . . 112

Chapter 9: Stories from My Main Roads Days 113
    My Charles Barton Story 113
        More About Charles Barton *114*
    My Russ Hinze Story 115
    Story About Organisational Identity 117
    My Chief Engineer Story 119
    Story About the Story Bridge 120
    Story About the Gateway Project. 122

Chapter 10: Learnings 125
    To Know But Not To Do 125
    Never Read a Speech 127
    The Winds Affect Our Moods 129
    How Much Mothers Do for Children 130
    Braking When Driving a Car 131
    Mode of Breathing 132
    A Learning from History 132
    A Learning from the Executive Dining Room . . . 133
    The Values Drummed into You in Childhood . . . 134
    The Throwaway Society 135
    A Learning About Modern Electronic Media . . . 136
    An Earlier Time of Decision and Action 137
    A Learning About Myself 138

Chapter 11: Near Misses 139
    Rolling a Watermelon Down a Slope 139

    Firing an Arrow 140
    Driving a Tractor into a Barbed-Wire Fence 142
    Driven Through Flood Water. 143
    Standing on the Running Board. 144
    Driving Back to Rockhampton for a Christmas Party . 145
    Falling Asleep at the Wheel 147
    Abseiling with the Road-Reform Team. 148

Chapter 12: Sayings 151

Chapter 13: Philosophy 155
    Humans and Planet Earth 155
    A Thought While on the Great Ocean Road 156
    My Attitude to Work. 156
        More About My Attitude to Work *158*
        Even More About My Attitude to Work *159*
    An Australian Ethos: Help your Neighbour 161
    The Pendulum Swings 161
    Life is a Strong Force 163
    The Stages Men Go Through as They Age 165

Chapter 14: Other Little Things That Have
        Stuck in My Mind 167
    Something Professor McKay Said 167
    Something a Lecturer at Purdue Said 168
    Something Our Headmaster Said at High School . . 168

Something Said By a Psychologist at a
Leadership Course 168
Something Said About Our Son 169
Something Our Eldest Grandson Said 169
Negotiations with Our Second London Grandson . . 169
Something Said By Our Youngest London Grandson 171
Message to Our Sydney Grandson on His
Tenth Birthday 171
Message from Our Only Granddaughter 173
Letter to a Nephew on His Twenty-first Birthday . . 173

Conclusion 179

Introduction

At this stage of my life, I find it fascinating how some little things have stuck in my mind. Often, when I'm having a conversation with someone, they will say something that triggers one of those thoughts, which leads me to share a story with them. And that in turn has led me to write this book about the little things that have stuck in my mind.

I was once asked to give an after-dinner speech at a Main Roads symposium, and I titled it 'Little Things That Stick in the Mind'. This was how I intended to commence my speech: 'Ladies and gentlemen, I have titled my speech "Little Things That Stick in the Mind", which is in contradistinction to a speech called "Things That Stick in a Little Mind", which is the other speech that I give!'

Partly because of the way the MC introduced me, I ended up changing the opening of my speech, but the audience still seemed to enjoy it very much; they certainly laughed a lot. It was perhaps the most successful speech I have ever given. Some of that content is included in this book.

It was difficult to decide how to organise the stories into chapters and sections. I started by arranging the content into categories: stories, memories, learnings, sayings, etc. The final result is a bit of a hotchpotch, but nevertheless I hope you enjoy reading the stories, and hearing about some of the little things that have stuck in my mind.

Chapter 1
GETTING STARTED

Great Motivators of Men

I once read that there are four great motivators of men. So, apart from women, that leaves only three: some men are motivated by money, some by power, and some by status (or prestige).

Looking back at this stage of my life, I can see that, perhaps unfortunately, I was never motivated by money. Down on the family farm, in north-east Brisbane, we had to work hard in the harvest season, but we never received pocket money.

Nor was I ever motivated by power. But I was motivated by status.

Where I grew up, in Lower Nudgee, our home had no flushing toilet. When I was a young child, our family relied on tank water; there was no piped water supply at that stage.

My mother grew up on a dairy farm in Lower Nudgee. She used to help her father and elder brother deliver milk to customers in the suburbs of Ascot, Hamilton and Clayfield (this was the era before pasteurised milk). Perhaps that helps to explain why I have lived, since Easter 1975, in a home in Ascot Street, Ascot. For me, an address in Ascot was a step up in social status from where I grew up.

When I joined the Department of Main Roads as a scholarship holder at the University of Queensland in 1964, the commissioner was a man named Charles Barton (later Sir Charles Barton). He was a tall, dignified man. I can recall thinking: *I'd like to be like that.*

With my Main Roads scholarship, I studied civil engineering at the University of Queensland. It disappointed me to see that although the senior medical students wore suits and ties, engineering students dressed in shorts and long socks.

As I reflect back on my career as a civil engineer, it is a disappointment to me that in our Australian culture we don't grant engineers the sort of status we award to top lawyers and doctors. But some cultures do: the Germans do, and the Russians also.

I once had a neighbour in Ascot Street who was of Russian descent. His father, he once told me, was very disappointed with him when he failed first-year engineering at the University of Queensland. He shifted to studying medicine and went on to become a prominent medical specialist.

But whenever I view the Gateway Bridges (i.e. the Sir Leo Hielscher Bridges), especially when I play golf at the Royal Queensland Golf Club, I think to myself: *You know, the people who can make that sort of thing happen deserve to be rated up with the best of any of them.*

I had a similar feeling when I watched the wonderful opening ceremony at the London Olympic Games, which I considered inspirational. Initially on the oval there were shepherds and sheep, as in the Agricultural Age. Then came great chimneys arising, signifying the Industrial Age.

At the end of that great performance the commentator said: 'The second greatest Englishman of all time, after Winston Churchill, was Isambard Kingdom Brunel, the great engineer of the Industrial Age.'

That gave me a good feeling.

Another Point of View

Towards the end of my career with Main Roads, senior management were concerned about the effect of the sudden retirement of a number of senior engineers who were nearing sixty-five years of age. Two colleagues and I were encouraged to step aside into mentoring-type roles and allow younger officers to take our positions.

The three of us were assigned offices on floor seven of the Spring Hill building, which was then the headquarters of the Department of Transport and Main Roads. Some colleagues used to refer to us as 'the three wise men'.

As part of this package, each of us was individually sponsored to have ten one-hour sessions with a man who described himself as a 'career architect'. He counselled people regarding 'transitions' in their careers.

Towards the end of my first counselling session this man gave me a questionnaire, asking me to complete it and bring it to our next meeting. It was something like a Myers-Briggs questionnaire, which sought to define personality types.

When I brought the completed questionnaire to my next session, he perused it and then said, 'Allan, what would you say are your primary motivators?'

'I have no idea,' I replied. 'What would you say they are?'

He responded quickly. 'Well, you only have one, and it's called pure challenge.'

I nodded and said, 'That might explain why I spend so much time doing Sudoku puzzles and cryptic crosswords.'

My German Connections

Where I grew up, in the Lower Nudgee district, there were many families with German-derived names, such as Schulz (one of my great-grandmothers was a Schulz), Wagner, Imhoff, Kunde, Kohle, Weller, Stegman, Grauf, Blinzinger, and so on.

Some were descendants of the German missionaries who had settled in the nearby area of Nundah in 1838. They were the first free white settlers in Queensland. However, the story of the Krosch family is different.

In Britain, there was a Queen Anne who had died without any successors. She'd had children, but none of them had survived her. So the British had to get a monarch from somewhere.

They chose George I, who came from the Province of Hanover in 1714. He was actually fiftieth in line to the throne, but they chose him because he was the nearest who was a Protestant. I learnt this when I visited the small, former Lutheran Church of St Georg's in Aldgate East, London, in 2017. An exhibition was taking place entitled '500 Years of German Protestants in Britain'. Whenever I visit London, where my eldest daughter and her family live, I always visit St Georg's.

My ancestor, Diederich Krösch, had moved from Hanover to London in 1790. Because the king had come from the province of Hanover, it became part of the British Empire—until the unification of Germany. Many people from Hanover came to live in the area near Whitechapel, which is near the port of London. It was the largest group of German-speaking people anywhere in the world outside of Germany. Many worked in the sugar-refining industry, turning the brown sugar, brought from the Caribbean, into white sugar.

Diederich Krosch became the licensee and operator of a hotel called The Castle. It is still there and operating, and located a short distance down the street from St Georg's.

On the rear wall inside St Georg's there is a plaque recognising Diederich Krosch, along with some others, for money they donated to help fund the operation of the school next to the church, attended by the children of German-speaking families living in the Whitechapel area. Diederich died in 1829, and in his will, he made provision for fifty pounds to be donated to the school. (I understand that in 1829 fifty pounds was a sizeable donation.)

One of Diederich's grandsons became a soldier in the British army, and in 1840 was sent to Sydney to help guard convicts. When his term expired, he did not return to Britain. He elected to remain in Australia and moved up to Brisbane. He is a great-great-grandfather of mine.

Some Germanic DNA

It is one of my sayings that when you have SCH on the end of your name you always have to be on time (it's in the genes).

My eldest daughter became a lawyer. After working in Brisbane for a time, she moved to a job in Sydney. Later we sponsored her to obtain a master's degree in law from Cambridge University. On completion of the course she got a job with one of the big law firms in London.

One morning she had organised a meeting, with ten people to attend, to commence at nine am. She arrived at quarter to nine and there was one man in the room. At one minute to nine, he was still the only other person present.

She said to him, 'Isn't this annoying? When you have SCH on the end of your name, you've always got to be on time.'

'Young lady, if you were a real German, as I am,' he replied, 'you would have been here since seven-thirty, as I have been.' (I think the man's name was something like Klaus von Schleiman.)

More on German Characteristics

Some years ago, my wife and I billeted two young German girls who had come to Brisbane for a week as members of the Mannheim Youth Orchestra. I had to drive them each morning to the Cultural Centre in the city and pick them up in the late afternoon or evening. One of them was not at all good at being on time, either leaving or being picked up. She never seemed to remember to take with her what was needed on the day, or ensure that she didn't leave something in the car when she disembarked.

I had formed the opinion that her surname didn't seem to be of Germanic origin. Towards the end of their stay with us, I said to this girl, 'I thought German people always have to be on time.'

'Oh, my father was Jordanian,' she replied.

Story of a German Character

Some years ago, I went to see Barry Gibb in concert at the Boondall Entertainment Centre. My wife didn't wish to go, so I booked a single seat on the floor area, not on the sloping side areas where

I find legroom lacking.

I got there quite early. The usher seated me third from the end of the row. The theatre was already nearly full, despite the early time, and there were just a few empty seats in our row, towards the middle.

I said to the guy in the fourth seat, 'Aren't we lucky we're here near the end and don't have to squeeze our way down to one of those empty seats?'

'You will have to speak more slowly,' he replied with a strong accent, 'I am from Germany.'

Chatting to him, I found out that he was from Cologne. He had seen on the internet that Barry Gibb was to perform at a concert in Brisbane. He had flown, specially, all the way from Cologne to Brisbane via Dubai, and had arrived in Brisbane earlier that day. Next morning, he was heading back to Cologne. He told me that he still preferred to listen to music on the old vinyl records.

The performance was magnificent. Barry Gibb sang for about two hours in his high falsetto voice. There were about ten musicians in his backing band. His son joined him in singing duets, and he was also joined by the daughter of one of his deceased brothers. His elderly mother was also in the audience.

When the concert was near the end, Barry departed the stage. The supporting artists commenced to sing (from the song 'Massachusetts') 'and the lights all went out …'

The lights did go out, and that's all we got of the song 'Massachusetts'.

The audience kept applauding. Barry came back on stage to sing a final song, and the concert ended. I expressed my disappointment that we had heard only one line from the song 'Massachusetts'.

I must have exchanged business cards with the gentleman from Cologne, because some weeks later I received an email from him requesting my street address. Another few weeks went by, and I got home from golf one day to find a huge cardboard carton on my front veranda. When I opened it up, I found a brand new German record player and two Bee Gees albums, one of which included the song 'Massachusetts'.

I had to think about how I could repay him. I found a store in Adelaide Street that has, one level up, a great range of vinyl records: 45s and 33s. I purchased two albums by The Seekers and sent them off to his Cologne address, with a message of thanks.

An Aryan Connection?

One evening, about a year after I retired, I attended an Engineers Australia event (I was still keeping up with continuing professional development).

After the presentation, refreshments were served.

When a young woman saw my nametag, she said, 'Mr Kor-osch, your name would be very well known in Iran, the country I am from. You are a descendant of Cyrus the Great.'

Now, I know that Germans are regarded as being of Aryan race, which means 'they came originally from Iran'. So I thought her suggestion might not be totally implausible.

I raised the matter with my brother, who studied German in high school, and has done an enormous amount of research into our Krosch family history.

'No, mate,' he said immediately, 'she's got it wrong. If our name was spelt Kor-osch then maybe, but no, she's got it wrong.'

In 2017 my wife, without consulting me, booked us on a group tour of Iran. During that tour we visited Persepolis and saw the Tomb of Cyrus. Even though I knew I was not a descendant of Cyrus, I must say that I enjoyed visiting his tomb rather more than would have been the case had I never heard that false story.

When we got back to London prior to returning home to Australia, I felt I should visit the British Museum and find the Cylinder of Cyrus. It is the oldest existing record of human writing, and has letters exposed on the outside of a cylindrical piece of stone.

Altogether, I spent about five hours, on foot, viewing some of the treasures in the British Museum. I left there with this thought in mind: *What a mighty empire the British Empire must have been to have brought so many great things back from so many countries around the world (whether rightly or wrongly).*

How could Britain have become a vassal state of the EU?

Footnote About Cambridge University

I was once speaking with an elderly gentleman who had been born and raised in England. He told me that he had studied for his university degree at Oxford. I told him that I had sent my daughter to do a master's degree at Cambridge.

'Oh, Cambridge,' he replied, 'I consider it to be one of the better of the new universities in Britain.'

Chapter 2

RIPOSTE; AND MY LINKAGE TO PHOENICIANS (THROUGH MARRIAGE)

Story from Our Wedding Reception

My wife and I were married in Rockhampton on 4 January 1969. At that time there were two barristers who were residents in Rockhampton: Mr Fred McGuire and Mr Bernie Treston. Both were present at the event.

In the year before I was married, I shared a rental house with three other single guys. Bernie Treston was one of them.

Fred McGuire was my wife's cousin, and he was the master of ceremonies at our wedding.

In his opening remarks, Fred quoted one of the great Greek philosophers: 'It is well for any man to marry. If you marry a good woman, you'll be very happy. And if you marry a bad woman, you'll become a philosopher—and that's good for any man!'

Instantly, the other barrister in town called out, 'Hey, Fred, which one are you?'

And almost instantly Fred replied (his wife being present), 'I am a happy philosopher.'

Story About Riposte

Many years later, there was an instance where I demonstrated riposte.

One evening, my wife and I were at a function where many were in attendance. Prior to dinner, all the guests were standing and chatting over a glass of wine and hors d'oeuvres.

I was talking to a gentleman, not realising that my wife was within earshot. In the course of conversation, I happened to say to him, 'I've been working for the same organisation for thirty-nine years, I've been married to the same woman for thirty-eight years, and we've been living in the same house for thirty-three years.'

Suddenly my wife was there beside me. 'Yes,' she said, 'and you're just dull and boring, and you don't like change.'

To which I replied, 'Lucky for you.'

The Only Real Wealth in Life

My late father-in-law was born in Lebanon. His family name was Jeha. He didn't marry until he was fifty. I used to spend a lot of time playing backgammon with him.

One Sunday when we were playing backgammon, he said to me, 'We Lebanese love our children more than ourselves, and our grandchildren more than our children.'

Perhaps he was giving me a hint to give him a grandchild.

My wife and I were married on 4 January 1969. Our first child was born on 28 May 1970. I can still remember ringing my wife's parents and telling them that she had given birth to a little girl. They rushed up to the hospital.

My father-in-law put his arm around his daughter as she lay in bed and said, 'Never mind, darling, he wouldn't have been a Jeha anyway.' (That is to say: 'Don't be disappointed you didn't give me a grandson.')

Often, when he visited our home to see his granddaughter, he would pat the baby and slip a five-pound note between her little fingers.

Sadly, he suffered a heart attack and passed away. His funeral was held on his granddaughter's first birthday; he lived to see one grandchild for one year.

Perhaps his attitude influenced my philosophy of life, which I express as follows: The only real wealth in life is grandchildren, and I'm in the lower-middle income bracket as I've only got five.

Perhaps one concept of eternal life is to have a little bit of your DNA running around on Earth long after you have gone.

Story About My Ability to Sell

When I was a boy down on the farm, people would sometimes call in at the packing shed at my grandparents' property looking to buy vegetables or fruit. There was never any bargaining, they were just charged what was the relevant wholesale market price at the time.

Soon after I met my future father-in-law, a very experienced and successful businessman of Lebanese birth, he said to me after playing a game of backgammon, 'Allan, can you sell?'

I replied, 'Well, if I had a shop and a customer came in wanting to buy, I reckon I could sell to them. I guess customers do come in looking to buy.'

The look on his face seemed to indicate that there was a lot more to being a successful salesman than I perceived.

Many years later, my son got involved in athletics at the Aspley Little Athletics Club. The club used to raise money by selling raffle tickets at the Homestead Hotel markets on Sunday mornings. I was assigned to sell tickets on several occasions, which wasn't an easy task. The prize was a cheap bottle of wine—with a fifty-dollar note around it secured by two rubber bands—and it was nowhere to be seen.

On my first occasion of selling these tickets I wondered

how I was going to do this. I was standing there with a handful of tickets, with a little money apron around my waist, saying, 'Aspley Little Athletics'.

An obese, middle-aged man was about to walk by. 'Sir,' I said, 'I can see that you've been an athlete, and perhaps—'

He responded instantly, cutting me off by saying gruffly, 'Why would you say that?'

'By the way you move, sir,' I said. 'And perhaps, having been an athlete yourself, you might be willing to buy some tickets for our Aspley Little Athletics' raffle.'

And he did. So I kept using that line as other people walked by. The funny thing was that the less likely it was true, the more successful it was. And I thought to myself: *You know, you could have been a salesman!*

Although it turned out that I could sell, I didn't really enjoy it. I didn't enjoy saying things to people that I knew were not true.

Stories About Jeha

My wife's family name was Jeha. It just so happens that 'Jeha' is a character in fables of the Phoenicians and Lebanese. There are many, many stories about Jeha in Lebanese tradition.

My father-in-law had told me, 'Lebanese are not Arabs; they are Phoenicians.'

I initially thought this meant that they came from North

Africa, like Hannibal, who came from Carthage. However, many years later, on a tour of Sicily, I learned that the Phoenicians came from an area that included parts of what are now Lebanon and Syria. They sailed vessels all around the Mediterranean Sea. I understand that they sailed to Portugal, where they purchased tin to use in making bronze.

Certainly, when my wife and I made a tour of Morocco in 2012 I heard stories about Jeha all across that country. My favourite story of Jeha was when he was a jester in the court of the king.

The king called Jeha into the throne room one morning and said, 'Jeha, I have been reading, and I have come across a sentence that, for the life of me, I just cannot understand. It is this: "The explanation was worse than the insult". I just can't understand how this could be. I will give you one week to come back and explain to me what this means, or else I'll have your head.'

So Jeha went off and spent the week racking his brain to try to provide an explanation for the king. But try as he might, he had no idea.

On the morning when he had to report to the king, he had no idea what he was going to say. But he was not an anxious type; he was a man who lived on his wits. So he went off to the palace in reasonably good spirits.

When he came into the throne room, the king wasn't there. He was out on the balcony, all rigged out with his crown and his ermine-trimmed robe, reviewing a passing parade of troops.

As Jeha headed towards the doorway to the balcony, he had a flash of genius. He walked quietly up behind the king and pinched him sharply on the buttocks.

The king whirled round and shouted, 'Jeha! I'll have your head for this.'

Jeha bowed and answered courteously, 'Pardon me, Your Majesty, I thought you were the queen.'

Story About Purchasing a Dress for My Fiancée

After meeting my future wife, I lived in Brisbane for the next twelve months while she lived in Rockhampton.

I drove up to Rockhampton to visit her for her birthday. To purchase a birthday present, I had gone to a shop in Brisbane called Marcia Gowns, where I sought to buy a dress. When I had chosen the style of dress I thought would be appropriate, the shop assistant asked me what size I was seeking. I had no idea, but there were some female customers in the store.

I pointed to one of them and said, 'About the size of that young lady over there.'

At that time I was a Main Roads scholarship holder, in my fourth year at the University of Queensland. In addition to having our university fees paid, we scholarship holders also received a modest living allowance. From memory, it was five pounds per week in the first year, and it increased slightly each succeeding year. In any event, the amount I paid for the dress was significant in relation to my scholarship living allowance.

I visited my fiancée and her family in Rockhampton and presented her with my gift. When she opened the present and saw the size of the dress, she showed it to her mother. They both burst out laughing. The size was so inappropriate that they found it ridiculous.

I felt embarrassed. When her father asked me where I had purchased it, I answered, 'Marcia Gowns.'

'Did you get a discount from Khalil Malouf?' he asked.

Khalil Malouf was the owner of Marcia Gowns. He was of Lebanese birth, and was well known to my future father-in-law. However, this was something I was not aware of, and I would never have contemplated asking for a discount from the owner of the business.

Can you imagine how I was feeling?

Story About Food Flavours

After we were married, my wife and I lived in Rockhampton. We often had Sunday lunches with her family. One Sunday an elder sister of her father was present for lunch. She was a lady in her seventies who had never married.

During the meal, some attention was focused on me due to my dislike of highly spiced food. My wife's elderly aunty made some mocking comments about the lack of flavour in the foods that Australians eat.

I retaliated by saying something along these lines: 'When you are a free people that hasn't been conquered, or 'under the heel of the Turk', you have always had good fresh food – never food that had deteriorated to the extent that it needed to be heavily spiced to make it palatable.'

She was outraged. 'He is insulting us,' she said. 'He is insulting us. But when you are perfectly confident you are correct, you cannot be insulted.'

Chapter 3

EXPERIENCES FROM THE UNITED STATES AND EUROPE

Stories from My Time at Purdue

In 1971–72, I was sponsored by Main Roads to study for a Master of Engineering degree at Purdue University, Lafayette, Indiana. I was accompanied by my wife and our first child, who was sixteen months old at the time.

At Purdue they had a foster-relative program, whereby foreign students could get to know American people, sometimes dining with them as guests in their homes. Our foster relatives were a retired professor, whose nickname was Van, and his wife Martha. I recall something Van said over lunch one day. (Van commenced many of his sentences with the word 'why'.)

'Why,' Van said, 'when Martha and I were married, we agreed that I would make all of the big decisions, and Martha would make all of the little decisions, and why, in forty-two years of marriage, we haven't had *one* big decision.'

Towards the end of winter, I said at another Sunday lunch, 'Well, Van, you don't seem to get a great deal of snow here in Lafayette.'

'Why, no,' he replied. 'Why, if I had to sweep the front path six times for snow this winter, that's all I would have swept it.'

And Martha chimed in, 'Oh, Van, you swept it many more times than six.'

And he answered, very politely, 'Well, it only seemed like six times.'

Stories from Travel in Europe in 1972

Following our travels across the US, and my meetings with various State Roads authorities, I was sponsored to attend a conference in London, as well as several meetings in London with Road Transport organisations.

Following those commitments, I had arranged to take several months of long-service leave and unpaid leave. My wife and I travelled extensively throughout the UK and elsewhere in

Europe, and made brief visits to Greece and Lebanon on our return journey to Australia.

My wife's mother and an aunty had come over to Lafayette and had taken our daughter back to Rockhampton.

Story from Versailles

We started our tour of mainland Europe in Paris. I still remember something that our guide said during our visit to the Palace of Versailles: 'Louis the fourteenth built it, Louis the fifteenth enjoyed it, and Louis the sixteenth paid for it!' (That is, with his head.)

Story from Norway

After we left Paris, we travelled to Amsterdam, then to Copenhagen, and then took a ferry to Norway. Something that happened in Norway has always stuck in my mind.

We had hired a little Volkswagen in Paris, to drive through a lot of Europe. We were travelling in Norway, and the winter was coming on. The little Volkswagen developed a problem with the clutch, and I could only start the car in gear.

We decided to take a ride on a big ferry, with the car on board, and travel down a large fiord called Sognefjord. When it came time to board, I started the car in gear, raced up the ramp onto the ferry deck and slammed on the brakes. The ferry could have carried many cars, but ours was the only one on deck. Nor were there any other passengers to be seen.

Looking up, I saw the ferry captain sitting in the wheelhouse, on a much higher level. He gave a signal for us to come up and join him. We climbed up many flights of stairs and did so. We spent the whole journey chatting to the captain as he steered the vessel.

I had not appreciated what a great mercantile shipping country Norway was. This man had sailed large merchant ships all around the world for many years, but now, as an old man, he just sailed this big ferry up and down the Sognefjord.

We chatted about many things.

A few days prior, there had been a referendum in Denmark to address the question of whether Denmark should join the Common Market (later to become the European Union). I asked what he thought about the proposal to form the EU.

He answered as follows: 'Well, I think English will be the language of commerce, German will be spoken by the military, and French will only be spoken in the bedroom!'

Driving in Germany

After our visits to Norway and Sweden, we took the Volkswagon on a ferry to Germany. We planned to drive to Berlin, but that meant going behind the Iron Curtain, the border between West Germany and East Germany. We weren't supposed to take the hired vehicle behind the Iron Curtain, but there was a transit road, by which foreigners could travel to West Berlin, and I judged that it would be reasonable to take that route.

We had been travelling for some time, frequently encountering soldiers along the way. Looking at the map, I thought I could see a better route than the one we were on that would take us to the gate of West Berlin, so I changed routes. But as we were approaching Berlin, I started to have doubts about whether we were approaching the gate of West Berlin or East Berlin.

I pulled up and asked some soldiers, pointing to the city gate. 'East Berlin or West Berlin?'

They answered in a way I couldn't understand at all.

I repeated: 'East Berlin or West Berlin?'

Again they answered with uninterpretable sounds.

I pointed again to the gate and asked, 'Willy Brandt Berlin?'

And they said, *'Nein, nein.'*

So I turned around and drove to the other gate, and we were safe.

That's the only time in my life I've ever needed to speak German.

Driving to Prague

After we left Berlin, we headed for Prague, Czechoslovakia. Along the way, an army vehicle travelling in the opposite direction caused a stone to hit our windscreen and smash a hole in it as big as a rock melon.

When we arrived in Prague, it was after nightfall and we had no hotel reservation. We decided we would have dinner first, and then endeavour to find accommodation. While we were dining, we saw two women at an adjacent table: a very attractive young woman and another woman we presumed to be her mother.

After some time, the young woman came over to our table. 'We understand you may need some help to find accommodation,' she said. 'I could assist you. When you have finished your meal, I will take you to a hotel.'

In conversation, we learned that she was a TV presenter and had learned English at school.

After our meal she came with us, in our car, to the hotel she had chosen. She asked me for some cash so she could secure the room booking. She then left, and we took our luggage up to the hotel room.

I was uncomfortable leaving the car on the street with a broken windscreen. Not only was it insecure, but to make matters worse it was in a location we were not supposed to have taken it to – behind the Iron Curtain.

I had the idea of loosening all the nuts on one of the car

wheels, so if anyone tried to steal the car the wheel would fall off. But with the small spanner I found in the boot of the car, I was unable to loosen any of the nuts. It was just as well we hadn't had a flat tyre in our travels.

I went back into the hotel foyer, only to find four very angry Russian military officers arguing with the hotel receptionist. It seemed there was some problem with their booking. The receptionist was looking up and down his reservation list, and seemed to be assuring them that they did not have a booking.

I formed the opinion that we possibly had the room the Russians had booked, and I quickly went up to the room and locked the door.

The next morning I found out where I could take the car to get a new windscreen fitted, which I did. I asked the mechanic if I could borrow a spanner. He must have thought it was a bit odd when I loosened all the wheel nuts with his spanner but retightened them with the small spanner from the boot of the car.

We then spent a few days sightseeing in Prague.

One day, when we were travelling in a rural area, I noticed something wrong with a rear wheel. It was wobbling terribly. I got out of the car with the intention of tightening the wheel nuts, but when I took off the hub cab, I was aghast. All but one of the studs from the wheel hub had broken off and were now in the hubcap (or so I thought).

I thought I had a major problem. Can you imagine my predicament? We were in a foreign country—one where we weren't supposed to have taken the car—in a rural area, and most of the studs on one of the wheel hubs had broken off.

But then I realised that the studs had *not* broken off. Unlike the cars I had driven in Australia, the wheels on this VW were not secured by nuts on studs, but rather by bolts that screwed into holes in the hub. All the bolts we required were there in the hubcap.

So I was able to jack up the car, put the rear wheel back on the hub, and then tighten all bolts on all four wheels—at least as well as I possibly could with my little spanner.

We had no further problems.

Story from Madrid

As part of our tour of Europe, we flew from Paris to Madrid. When we disembarked and came into the airport terminal, whom should I see waiting but a person who had been a classmate at Purdue, Indiana. His name was Miguel.

It was just a chance meeting. Miguel was there to meet Professor Goetz and his wife. Professor Goetz had taught at Purdue, and Miguel had been in one of his classes. (I had been in other classes with Miguel.)

We spent some time with Miguel and the Goetzes, visiting famous museums and art galleries. The El Prado was one of them.

Mrs Goetz insisted on pronouncing Miguel's name 'Michael'.

On one occasion, when we were viewing a famous painting by El Greco, Mrs Goetz said, 'Michael, what does "El" mean?'

'You see, Mrs Goetz,' Miguel replied, 'El Greco was not Spanish, he was Greek. He was known as "the Greek" and "El" means "the".'

My wife and I then hired a car and drove around Spain, visiting lots of places, including Grenada. But perhaps we were becoming 'over-toured' and didn't see all that we should have.

When we got back to Madrid, we caught up briefly with Miguel prior to flying out to Athens. 'What did you think of the Alhambra?' he asked me.

'Is that what we were supposed to see in Granada?' I replied.

He was flummoxed. 'Oh, you have missed the most important thing in all of Spain.'

Chapter 4

MEMORIES OF FISHING AND TENNIS

Fishing at Clairview

When I was in my early thirties, I played tennis with three other guys on a private grass court in Ascot. We'd play on Wednesdays, in the late afternoon.

One of the guys used to go on fishing trips on the Great Barrier Reef. On one such occasion, on the drive back he noticed that a section of the Bruce Highway between Marlborough and Sarina was being relocated to a new route closer to the coast. He realised that it would be the first place, north of Brisbane, from where the Pacific Ocean could be seen from the Bruce Highway.

He bought a house right on the beach, in a village called Clairview, south of Sarina.

A bit later, during a depression in the sugar-cane industry, he bought about a thousand acres of rubbish country from a struggling cane farmer. From memory, this parcel of land was about twenty-five kilometres north of Clairview. With this parcel of land, he had about twenty kilometres of private beach frontage to the Broad Sound in a remote area south from Bluewater Creek.

On a couple of occasions he had his tennis mates join him on a fishing trip for about a week. The tidal range in that area of the Broad Sound is about six metres, due to the surge of the tide coming down the inlet.

The fishing was done with nets, set square to the coastline. On our first fishing trip, he took us up to the fishing area in the late afternoon, to put the nets in place. We had to be back there very early the next morning, before daylight, when the tide was at a low level. The fish had to be taken out of the nets so they weren't left on the sand in daylight, otherwise sea eagles would peck them, and they would be inedible.

It was wintertime, and when we got there the next morning it was pretty cold. At the first net we found some large flathead and king salmon. We had to disentangle them from the net in the dark, with just the light from the headlights of the four-wheel-drive vehicle to assist us.

At the second net it was much the same. Some more flathead and king salmon.

As we approached the mouth of Bluewater Creek to check the third net, the sun had not yet risen but there was a bit of a red glow in the eastern sky. The headlights shone out to sea, and we saw a silvery flash on the sandbar.

It was the reflection from a big barramundi.

You might not think it would be exciting to catch a fish in a net, but in this case it was.

We also checked some crab pots we had positioned in the mouth of Bluewater Creek the previous evening. We had used a small dinghy to tie the ropes, attached to the crab pots, to tree branches just above water level. Now, at low tide, those branches were about six metres above water level.

There were some large mud crabs in the pots for us to take home, along with the fish.

When we got back to our friend's house in Clairview, his old neighbour Cec came over to see how we had fared. Cec was a retired coalminer. He used to work at a coalmine near Ogmore, back in the days of the steam trains.

We asked Cec if he had some scales we could use to weigh the large barramundi. He gave us what he had, but they were not able to do the task.

Our host said to Cec, 'What weight do you think the barramundi would be, Cec? Would it be thirty pounds?'

'It's a pretty good fish,' Cec replied, 'but I don't think it's quite thirty pounds. Maybe in the high twenties. But it's nothing like the biggest one we ever caught in the Styx River near Ogmore when I was a boy. And we caught it in water only six feet deep. The only trouble was that all its back was sunburnt and all its belly was gravel-rashed. But at least we never had to wash up the dishes again after that. Every time we had a meal we just used the scales for plates.'

Cooking Mud Crabs at Clairview

On our trip up to Clairview, our host had insisted on stopping at Nambour to buy some garlic and ginger, to be used for cooking mud crabs.

I knew a bit about catching and cooking mud crabs. When I was a boy down on our farm, we would catch mud crabs in a tributary of the Serpentine Creek, which was within walking distance from the back boundary of the farm.

We'd take the crabs home in large hessian bags, separated from each other by mangrove branch clippings. We'd fill the big copper that Mum used for laundry purposes, and when the water was boiling, we'd kill the crabs with a sharp metal spike and put them in the copper to cook.

Our host had a completely different way of cooking crabs. He steamed them. He had a big pot, into which he placed a 'fake bottom', a little bit of water, and finely chopped garlic and ginger.

He asked me to kill the crabs and remove their top shells. Removing the shells is a much harder task with uncooked crabs than it is with cooked crabs. I thought his method of cooking crabs was a bit over the top, so I cooked a few of them in boiling water as we'd always done down on the farm.

That evening we sat down to eat the mud crabs. I had some that had been cooked his way and some that were cooked my way. There was no comparison. The flavour of his steamed crabs was far superior to those I'd cooked by simply boiling them in water.

Memories of Tennis

In my early thirties I used to play tennis regularly with my three fishing friends in Ascot, and also with a team in the Brisbane Night Fixtures competition.

I was no great tennis player. I'd never played competitively as a child, and never had any coaching. I did not have a good service action or good groundstrokes, especially backhand. But I was good at volleying. I only ever played doubles.

One night I was about to go and play in the Night Fixtures competition. Before I left home, I rang my mother to hear about the outcome of a visit to the doctor she'd had that day. She told me that her GP had given her the all-clear, and I went off to tennis feeling very happy. The GP's diagnosis proved to be incorrect. My mother actually had ovarian cancer, although she did manage to live for another twenty-five years after it was treated.

But that night, as I headed off to tennis after hearing the misdiagnosis, my mind was in a very special place. I was 'in the zone'. Everything I did on the court was spot on. Every serve was on the service line. Every lob was on the baseline. It was the best tennis I had ever played.

The only problem was that next morning I couldn't bend my elbow. I had developed tennis elbow, and it took about nine months to heal. On my doctor's advice, I had to massage the sore spot, transversely, with the thumb of my left hand. I did it so diligently that I started to wear away the skin, until I began to apply some lubricant to avoid skin damage.

From that experience, I had a learning about how the state of mind can affect performance in sport and athletics.

Chapter 5

SINGING AND JOKE TELLING

Becoming a Member of the Brisbane Club

My wife, our daughters and I moved into our home in Ascot Street, Ascot in Easter 1975. Some months later we had become friends with neighbours up the street. I have fond memories of singalongs around their pianola.

The husband was a member of the Brisbane Club, and in due course he was kind enough to nominate me for membership in the club. In those times it took years on the waiting list to become a member.

I think it was about 1979 when I got a phone call at work from the club manager, Mr Joe Borsellino. 'Mr Krosch,' he said, 'your name is coming up before the nomination committee tonight. Could I just clarify a few things? Now, you work at Main

Roads, is that right?'

'Yes,' I replied.

'Now, first you have the minister, and then you have the commissioner. Could you tell me, er, where do you come?'

'Could we start from the bottom and work up?' I said.

'Well, could you become the commissioner, do you think?'

'Yes, I think I could.'

And though I never did become commissioner, I have been a member of the Brisbane Club for about forty years.

In those days, the club would have Friday evening dining events, with entertainment, every four to six weeks. If you didn't book the day after the invitation came in the mail, you'd likely not be able to gain admission. (Of course, in those times there weren't nearly so many restaurants in Brisbane as there are now.)

There would be evenings like a French Night or an Italian Night, with dining and entertainment in the relevant theme. There would also be events such as a Gilbert & Sullivan Night.

My wife and I would never miss these events. We'd generally know about ten or twelve of the other couples present through the connections we had made, which were often related to our children's schooling or other activities. It became something of a social hub for us.

Story About Gentlemen's Clubs in Brisbane

When I became a member of the Brisbane Club, three of the leading gentlemen's clubs in Brisbane were the Queensland Club, the Brisbane Club and Tattersall's Club. (I should perhaps mention that the Brisbane Club allowed women to become members some twenty years ago. Tattersall's Club did so only in recent times.)

An elderly gentleman once told me that when the Queensland Club was first established it was a club for the judiciary and the landed gentry; the Brisbane Club was a club for businessmen and working professionals; and Tattersall's Club was a club for entrepreneurs and the racing set.

It is my understanding that at the Queensland Club in the early 1900s it was considered inappropriate to discuss business issues. And I also understand that the Brisbane Club was formed by some gentlemen who left the Queensland Club because they wanted to belong to a club where business *could* be discussed in the club.

In my early years of membership at the Brisbane Club, I didn't attend lunches in the dining room very often. I was too busy at work. But when I did attend, the main dining room was always full until about two pm, after which it was nearly empty. In those years, solicitors and accountants could take their clients to lunch as a tax-deductible expense, but, being working professionals, they had to get back to their offices soon after two o'clock.

On rare occasions I was invited to dine, as a guest, at Tattersall's Club. The dining room there was always full, and was still nearly full well into the afternoon.

Memories of Prince Philip

I remember well the official opening of the Brisbane Club's new premises at 241 Adelaide St, following the construction of the new building on the site.

Prince Philip had been invited to officially open the new premises. He and the Queen had been on their liner, the HMS *Britannia*, up at the Great Barrier Reef prior to the official visit to Brisbane. Prince Philip had flown down to Brisbane that morning to be present at the official opening.

I was in a group conversing with Prince Philip when a club member, just to make conversation, asked him, 'Prince Philip, how was your flight down this morning?'

Prince Philip looked him in the eye and replied, 'Have you ever been on an aeroplane?'

'Yes,' the man replied, somewhat taken aback.

'Well,' said Prince Philip, 'it was just like that.'

The man who had asked the question, whose name was of Irish origin, was not happy to be spoken to in that manner.

Some days later, the Queen and Prince Philip were aboard HMS *Britannia*, which was moored at Hamilton Wharves.

The rector at St Augustine's Anglican church in Racecourse Road had invited Prince Philip to attend a Sunday service and read a passage from the Bible. Word went around about this visit, and that it would be necessary to obtain a ticket to reserve an allocated seat in the church. Some of the locals who weren't regular attendees at church services got in early and obtained tickets. Other stalwarts of the congregation missed out. I understand it caused some dissension in the community at the time.

On the day, Prince Philip sent his apologies and did not attend.

I was not present at the church, but I was told that the rector chose for the Bible reading a section that included the phrase: 'Put not your faith in princes.'

Music of the Century

In the lead-up to the New Year of 2000, a few fellows from the Brisbane Club choir decided to organise a private event to see in the New Year. Michael Evans, Collin Myers and I were the organisers. We titled the concert performance, Music of the Century.

We hired a room at the Cultural Centre, and had about a hundred and twenty attendees, if I recall correctly. We engaged a band, the leader of which may have been Lockie Thompson. We also engaged some professional singers.

The music we chose consisted of hit songs from each decade of the twentieth century. The first collection of songs was referred to as 'the pre-First World War bracket'. The first three songs in this bracket were 'Alexander's Ragtime Band' (Irving Berlin 2005), 'Pack Up All Your Troubles' and 'Tipperary'. The songs were to be sung by men from the Brisbane Club choir: six tenors, and six basses (which included me).

Now, nearly everyone knows the words to the chorus of 'Alexander's Ragtime Band', but not necessarily the verse, so we decided to sing the verse like this:

First couplet	Tenors
Second couplet	Basses
Third couplet	Tenors
Fourth couplet	Basses

Then we would all come in for the chorus.

It was decided that we would not have songbooks, which meant we had to learn the words by heart.

The evening was a splendid occasion.

When the Brisbane Club choristers began to sing the first bracket, starting with 'Alexander's Ragtime Band', it started well. But when we basses were due to sing the fourth couplet, every last one of us forgot the lyrics and nobody at all came in. That is, not until the chorus.

Being something of a perfectionist, it was a huge embarrassment to me. I don't think I got over it until Easter time. But on reflection, I had a significant learning from that experience, which I express like this: 'When you stuff up, the audience actually likes you more. It shows that you're human.'

Piano Story

I never learnt to play the piano when I was young. Some months after moving into our home in Ascot Street, neighbours down the street invited us to Sunday lunch. During the conversation, another guest, who was not a neighbour, mentioned that he was learning to play the piano as a mature-age student. He was being taught by a professional pianist, Mr Dick do Rozario, who played for many years at the Camelia Room restaurant in Queen Street.

After lunch, I asked the guest to play the piano for me. At first he declined. He said he never played for others, only for himself. However, he did eventually agree to play a few songs on the hosts' piano. I thought to myself: *If I could play like that, it would certainly be good enough for me.*

I asked him for contact details for his teacher and arranged to have a weekly morning lesson in the studio of Dick do Rozario, which was one level above ground in what later became the Myer Centre. I would park my car near Festival Hall and walk two blocks to the studio.

Dick do Rozario told me he was born in Hong Kong to Portuguese parents and had grown up in Vietnam. He had been sent to Paris as a young man, where he obtained a master's qualification in playing, composing and arranging music. He then went to New Orleans, where he had played for some of the great singers. And then he came to Brisbane, where he had played for many years at the Camelia Room restaurant in Queen Street.

I had to bring to my first lesson an empty music manuscript book. He wrote on the top of the first page 'Peggy O'Neill'. Then he wrote the notes for the melody of line one. On the last page he wrote down the notes of some chords.

I had to go home, ink in what he'd written in pencil and practise for one hour per night.

His method was something like the Scheffé method, with melody notes to be read and played, but the supporting chords played by the left hand from memory.

For each of the next three weeks, he added a further line to 'Peggy O'Neill' until the song was complete. Thereafter, he gave me a new song each week. Looking back, I think they were all hit songs from the 1920s, with titles like 'Alice Blue Gown', 'It Happened in Monterey' and so on.

They were all played in 3:4 time. They were played in various keys, and the number of chords, which I had to memorise, continued to increase.

At each weekly lesson I'd have to start by playing the song he had written in at the preceding lesson. As I played, I had to periodically turn my face to him and smile.

He told me that in four years he'd have me playing in pubs; however, after just six months, he was diagnosed with lung cancer and my lessons ceased. But I kept practising one hour per night.

Then, months later, just after New Year, I got a phone call from his wife. She said that he had decided to close his studio in the city, and just have four students who would come to their home for lessons, and he'd like me to be one of them. She asked if I could come next Monday

'Certainly,' I replied. I was delighted.

The following Sunday evening she phoned again. 'My husband is not feeling well,' she said. 'Could you come next Monday?'

But next Monday was the day of his funeral.

I attended his funeral, where his son played the organ during the service.

I contacted the man who had originally introduced me to Dick do Rozario, and borrowed some of the music books he had developed while learning to play. I kept practising one hour a night for another few years, but I felt I wasn't getting anywhere so I gave it all away.

Many years later, my father spent the last year of his life in the aged-care facility at Hilltop Gardens. There was a piano there, and often when I visited on a Sunday I took note of all the people sitting around but no one was playing the piano. So I decided I would play it, by ear.

It was the only place where my playing was ever appreciated. Perhaps it was an indication of how bad the residents' dementia had become. Although I'm no great pianist, I can play by ear songs that I know, as long as I play them in the scale of F, and only using three chords with my left hand: F, C and B flat.

My father was in a room with four beds. A man opposite him had suffered from a stroke, and although his speech was very limited, he was able to let me know how much he enjoyed hearing me play 'Jamaican Farewell'.

Ross, the man in the bed next to my father, also had difficulty speaking clearly. One Sunday, I played the piano at lunchtime and returned to visit Dad in the evening.

Ross said to me, with difficulty, 'I really enjoyed your playing.'

'Oh, Ross, I'm no great pianist,' I replied, 'I only ever had twenty-six half-hour lessons.'

'Ah, but you played with soul,' he replied.

Which is perhaps the kindest thing anyone ever said to me.

On another Sunday, I was playing hymns and Ross was singing along. When I finished playing I went over to Ross.

'I can see that as a child you must have been sent to Sunday school,' I said to him. 'I'll test your knowledge of the scriptures. There were three occasions when something was lost, and it caused great sadness, but when it was found there was great happiness.'

'I'll give you a few clues,' I said. 'The first was the lady who lost a coin from her bracelet. She swept the floor of her home until she found it. The second was the shepherd who came home in the dark with his flock of sheep and found a sheep missing. He went back and searched for it until he found it.'

I then said, 'What was the third one?'

He answered immediately: 'The Prodigal Son.'

Some months later Ross passed away. When I read his funeral notice in the newspaper, I learned that he had been an international Christian missionary—and there I had been, testing his knowledge of the Bible.

Story of Hymn Singing

I was raised in the Methodist religion and loved the Wesleyan hymns. Many years later, my children attended Sunday school at St Augustine's Anglican church. Monthly, my wife and I would attend the Sunday morning church service, which the children from Sunday school also attended.

My eldest daughter once asked me what my religion was.

'They don't have my religion anymore,' I replied, meaning that there was no Methodist church anymore because it had become part of the Uniting Church.

At the Anglican services I attended, I would look through the hymn list to see if I knew any from my youth. Only rarely did I see any familiar hymns, and they were invariably played in some obscure tune, not the tune I associated with them.

Then one Sunday morning a fine old Wesleyan hymn was being played to the tune that I knew. So I was singing along as loudly as I could, which wasn't very loud but apparently it was louder than others nearby.

My eldest daughter, who was then about eleven years old, tugged on the sleeve of my jacket and said, 'Dad, Dad, shush, you're embarrassing me.'

'Don't be silly,' I said. 'That's how we always sang in the Methodist church.'

She grimaced. 'Well, I can see why they don't have that church anymore.'

More on Music

In my latter career at Main Roads, I came across what I thought was a very nice saying. I paid privately to have the words set in a nice font and framed. It hung on the wall of my office for a few years pre-retirement. Nearly everyone who visited my office for the first time would comment on it. These were the words:

'God respects me when I work;

But he loves me when I sing.'

Which, of course, is not to skite about my singing talent but to point out the importance of happiness. When we're singing, it usually means we are happy, even if there is truth in the words: 'The sweetest songs are those that tell of saddest thoughts.'

The Physics of Music

I once read a book called *The Physics of Music*, which claimed that Western music has three dimensions.

First there is melody, which has been sung by folk singers

for thousands of years.

The second dimension is harmony, which started with choirs singing in Christian churches in the Middle Ages. First there were two parts, sung by men and boys, and later there were four parts: soprano, alto, tenor and bass.

The third dimension is rhythm, for example, the rhythm that is intrinsic to the music of the West Indies.

When I reflect on my own singing, I think God gave me a good sense of melody. If someone were to hit a note on a piano, without being able to see it I could find the key. Not immediately, perhaps, but certainly after trying a few keys. I do have to acknowledge, however, that God gave me very little sense of harmony, and no innate sense of rhythm.

A Memory for Lyrics

In the late 1990s, the director general of Main Roads encouraged members of the executive management group to attend courses on the subject of experiential leadership development. The courses were held for senior officers of Queensland State Government departments.

I attended one such course with several colleagues, together with officers from a range of other departments. The course was based on a branch of psychology called neurolinguistic programming (NLP).

One aspect of NLP theory is that the brain is like a computer, with a central processor and a memory data bank. We access that memory data bank via one of our senses. Some people access memory by the sense of seeing (i.e. photographic memory), some by hearing, and some by feeling (i.e. emotions).

One day during the course, a colleague said to me, 'Allan, I think you must access memory through the auditory channel.'

'I have no idea,' I replied. 'Why do you think that?'

'You know the words of so many songs.'

And I do.

In the past, when I have attended conferences or courses that have involved overnight stays, I have endeavoured to get a singalong going. I have some very fond memories of them.

I would normally start with a few Scottish songs like 'I Belong to Glasgow', 'Roaming in the Gloaming', 'Mull of Kintyre' and 'The Northern Lights of Old Aberdeen'.

Then we'd go across the Irish Sea and sing 'Danny Boy' and 'Galway Bay'.

Then we'd go down to the Caribbean for 'Jamaica Farewell' and 'Sloop John B'.

Then perhaps some Johnny Cash songs like 'I Walk the Line' and 'Fulsome Prison'.

From there, the singing would just carry on.

Story About Telling Jokes on the Radio

My second daughter had become a radio presenter for the ABC at Longreach. She rang me at work one Tuesday, just after nine am, and asked for my help.

'Can you help me, Dad?' she said. 'You know I do the breakfast show. Well, every morning I get someone to phone in and tell a joke on air. But today I don't have any listeners willing to do it. Could you help me with a joke on air?'

I was hesitant. After all, I was a senior executive in the Queensland Public Service. Anyhow, I did it for her.

Two days later she rang me again with the same request, and again I obliged her.

The following weekend was a long weekend, and the idea came into my mind that I should write down all the jokes I knew. To save time, I just wrote down the punchline of each joke. I kept adding to the list, and over that long weekend I wrote down the punchlines of a hundred and sixty-eight jokes.

I thought about publishing a book of jokes, but there was a problem with that idea. Although the jokes were humorous, there were some with which I would not have wanted my name to be associated. Then I had the idea that perhaps I could get someone else to put their name on the book, as author, and perhaps take only a small percentage of the net revenue from sales.

In the end I never got around to writing the book, let alone having it published.

The funny thing is that after so many years I recently came across my list of the punchlines of a hundred and sixty-eight jokes. Disappointingly, with some of them I can't recall the joke leading up to the punchline.

Chapter 6

MEMORIES

Memories from Skiing

My first experience of snow skiing was at Smiggins Hole in about 1978.

During our honeymoon on Norfolk Island in 1969, my wife and I had met a wonderful couple called Jim and Luba Simpson. Jim was a keen skier, and years later he encouraged us to bring our family to join his family on a skiing holiday. We then had two daughters, aged about eight and five.

When I was skiing on that trip, I wore a bright yellow beanie.

My eldest daughter was in a ski-school group with a very strict female Austrian ski instructor. In one of the lessons, she was not paying attention.

The instructor spoke sharply to her. 'Young lady, pay attention and learn to ski properly while you're young so that when you grow up you won't be skiing like that man over there.'

My daughter looked around, saw my beanie and knew it was me.

During that holiday at Smiggins Hole, I was skiing on the beginners' slope, near where the T-bar was towing skiers up the hill. A woman was coming up on the T-bar as I was crossing her path. I could easily have skied ahead of her or behind her, but somehow I lost my way and completely bowled her over.

Now, there's not much chivalry on the slopes, but I sidestepped my way back up to her, helped her gather her possessions and reached out to help lift her to her feet.

She took my hand, looked me straight in the eye and said, 'Well, you could at least have looked like Robert Redford.'

Skiing in Colorado

On one occasion, my wife and I were privileged to be included in a group of ten Brisbane people who went on a skiing trip to Vaile, Snowmass and Aspen Highlands in Colorado.

One day while skiing, my wife had a serious fall. It subsequently required knee surgery, although she was able to postpone that until returning to Brisbane. But what sticks in my mind about that incident is that a young man came up to her and said, respectfully, 'Ma'am, I can be your witness.'

That was our first experience of how litigious a society the United States was to become.

I can cite another example, this time from a 1986 visit to a Road Authority in the US. They had replaced the word 'guardrail' in all their manuals and specifications with the word 'guiderail'. This was to avoid being sued by any driver who had crashed off the roadway and claimed the railing had not adequately 'guarded' them.

Reflections on Skiing

For my seventieth birthday, we had a dinner party in the main dining room of the Brisbane Club.

In my speech I said, 'If I could live my life again there are a few things I'd do differently. One, I would learn to speak four or five languages. And two, I would do more snow skiing.'

In my experience, nothing takes the mind to a higher level than skiing in good snow on a perfectly still day.

Jim Simpson – a New South Wales Patriot

Jim was a great character and a wonderful friend. It is a great shame that his life was far too short. Jim always had you laughing with his remarks. He was a great New South Wales patriot.

He would say things like: 'Here we are in New South Wales, shearing sheep as big as whales.'

Or: 'The only good thing to ever come out of Queensland is the road to New South Wales.'

On State of Origin nights, I would always ring him at halftime. It was great to do so when the Maroons were leading, as they usually were in those years.

Jim's wife Luba told me that on the occasions when they drove up to Queensland to visit us, as they approached the New South Wales/Queensland border, Jim would say to the family, 'We're crossing the border into Queensland. Please set your watches back one hour, and your minds back ten years.'

Story from Expo 86

In 1986, Main Roads sponsored me to attend a conference in Vancouver, Canada, and also make visits to a number of Road Authorities in parts of Canada and the US. The conference occurred when Expo 86 was on, the theme of which was Transport and Communications.

At our private expense, my wife accompanied me on this trip. After the conference finished we could attend the Expo. We had just one more day in Vancouver, so we had to think carefully about how much time to invest in queuing up to gain admission to which pavilions. I made the judgement that we should be prepared to invest considerable time to get into the IBM pavilion, where I expected to learn something about advances in computer technology.

We finally got inside the pavilion and the show started. There was an old Native American man standing at the front of the stage. A bit of smoke was coming from his fire.

'Oh, it's all very worrying, this modern technology,' he said, 'but my grandmother had a saying: "Wouldn't it be wonderful if you could have a magic canoe. You could step into your canoe, think about where you wanted to go, take one paddle stroke and you'd be there. Life and the freedom to move are as one."'

There now seemed to be more smoke coming from his fire.

He spoke about what life was like in British Columbia before the white man came. 'The salmon swam in the rivers,' he said. And suddenly there were salmon swimming in the smoke from the fire.

'The wild ducks flew in the sky.' And suddenly there were ducks flying in the smoke.

The images were created by something called 'holography', which involved intersecting laser beams. That was where the technology came in. But his message was a simple though significant one: life and the freedom to move are as one.

That message is of special significance for anyone who spent part of their career, as I did, involved in building roads in rural areas, where graziers were very pleased to get bitumen-sealed roads to connect them to towns and cities. As a young engineer,

I would visit graziers who were about to be affected by planned upgrading to country roads. I was always welcomed with a cup of tea and scones.

I would sometimes be asked: 'When are we going to get the tar?'

That type of reception was very different to the ones I received when I became involved in the planning and design for the Northern Freeway and had to visit people whose homes were to be taken by compulsory government acquisition.

My Female Neighbour's View About Women's Brains

About twenty years ago, my wife had a problem with blurred peripheral vision. She went to see an optometrist, who referred her to a brain specialist. After a CT scan, then an MRI, she was diagnosed with a meningioma on the edge of her brain. It was very worrying.

She had the meningioma removed and was still in hospital when, a few days later, I was on the footpath in front of our home.

A lady who lived nearby came past and said, 'How's your wife?'

'She's fine,' I replied. 'There was no malignancy, and they only had to remove a very small part of her actual brain.'

'What part was that?' the lady asked.

'The part that controls kindliness to husbands and patience with children,' I replied.

She instantly responded: 'Oh, that's a very small part of any woman's brain.'

My Experience on Sentry Duty in Oaklands Parade

My son went to high school at Churchie. A school dance was convened, and girls came from other Anglican schools. Parents were requested to take on various roles, and I volunteered to perform sentry duty.

On the evening of the dance, I was assigned a position in Oaklands Parade. Those on sentry duty were instructed not to leave their positions until the event had concluded.

The dance commenced at seven pm. It was a cool night, with winter coming on.

As time passed, I thought: *How am I going to do this? It's so boring.* I looked at my watch. It was twenty minutes past seven.

After an hour had seemed to pass I looked at my watch again. It was now seven-thirty.

Ignoring instructions, I walked down the street about fifty metres and said to another man on sentry duty, 'Isn't this boring?'

'I don't find it so,' he replied.

We got chatting. He told me he was a private detective and often had to spend long periods 'on watch' in secluded locations, waiting to see if a certain person came to, or left, a particular site. He said that he had trained his mind not to notice the passage of time. He said he also had the ability to fall asleep anywhere, anytime.

'I could lie down on that concrete step there,' he said, 'without any pillow or blanket, and be fast asleep in no time.'

He also told me that he had never experienced the emotion of fear. He mentioned some of the things he had been engaged to do as a private detective.

There was one instance where a married couple had split up, and one of them had taken their child and returned to their home country, which was behind the Iron Curtain. He had gone to that country, found the child, and secretly brought the minor back to Australia with him.

To have never experienced the emotion of fear seemed remarkable to me. In those days, if whilst driving my car I had glanced in the rear-vision mirror and seen a policeman on a motorcycle behind me, my heart rate would have sped right up.

I wondered whether the detective did not have a gland that releases adrenalin.

I returned to my position and remained there until the dance ended.

While my son was at Churchie, at all future dances I volunteered to count the money.

Memories of *Cloud Street*

Many years ago, my wife and I went to the Queensland Performing Arts Centre to see a stage performance of *Cloud Street*, a play based on a book written by Tim Winton. We had to be seated by six pm, when the play commenced.

The story was about two families living in a house in Perth in the years of the Great Depression. The house was divided into two parts on either side of a central hallway. The two families lived on either side of the corridor. In one family there was a young man in his late teens whose nickname was Fish. He was a bit of an oddball character, if my memory is correct.

After two acts of the play, we all went out to dinner. That was part of the package. Then we all went back into the theatre and watched two more acts of the play.

Then we all went out for supper, which was also part of the package. Following supper, we all went back to see the final act of the play.

Altogether, there were about five hours of on-stage performance. The play ended at about midnight.

I have never read the book *Cloud Street*, and nor is my memory good enough to remember the story. But on the night of the show, it was my perception that Fish's life would not have ended well.

There was a line at the end of that great saga of a play that has stuck clearly and firmly in my mind: 'It is the role of the strong to protect the weak, and the role of the weak to teach the strong.'

Memories from My Time at Cribb Island State School

My family lived in Lower Nudgee, but my siblings and I attended the Cribb Island State School during our primary years. Nudgee State School was actually closer, but the Cribb Island bus service ran past our farm and past Cribb Island State School.

I should mention in passing that when my brother Neil was in grade eight, Barry Gibb of the Bee Gees was in his class. The Gibb family first lived at Cribb Island, after they emigrated from Britain and before they moved to Redcliffe.

I should also mention that in the mid-1970s the whole Cribb Island community was displaced when the government requisitioned all of the land to build the new Brisbane airport. All the farms in Lower Nudgee were also taken, including the Krosch family farms. A stage play called *Cribbie* was later created to tell the story of how a whole community was taken away. If you ever have a chance to see it, do not miss it. It is one of the finest stage plays that I have ever seen.

When I was in grades seven and eight (1958 and 1959), the schoolboys from the Cribb Island State School would travel by bus to the Breakfast Creek State School to attend classes in woodwork and metalwork. This happened one day per week for part of the year.

After class, when the boys were waiting to catch the bus back to Cribb Island, they would go into a store near the bus stop that sold food and drink. While one of the group got the attention of the shopkeeper, some of the boys (but never me) would rake lollies and sweets from trays on the counter into the front pockets of their woodwork aprons.

Also when I was in grade seven and eight, I was a member of the Cribb Island State School cricket team. We played matches against teams from other schools such as Nudgee State School and Sandgate State School. Each match was played over two consecutive Friday afternoons.

I have a particular memory about one match we played against Sandgate State School in 1959. At stumps on day one, the Cribbie players boarded a train at the Sandgate railway station to head back to the Nudgee railway station. From there they would ride their bicycles back home.

As the departing train was approaching a level crossing, the boys on the train saw all the Sandgate players standing, astride their bikes, close to the railway gate that had been closed for the train to pass through (this was before the age of boom gates).

Most of the Cribbie players (me excluded), stood up and stuck their heads out the train windows, and as they passed the Sandgate players, they spat on them. Or, to use the terminology of the time, they 'gollied' on them.

On the following Friday, day two of the match, surprisingly the Sandgate players made no mention of the terrible conduct of the Cribbie players the Friday before.

I can't recall which team won the match, but at the end of the game players from the two teams shook hands and set off home as they had after day one. When the train was approaching the level crossing, all the Sandgate players were there again, astride their bikes, just as they had been the week before. It seemed that they were slow learners.

Most of the Cribbie players (but not me) again put their heads out the windows of the train with the intention of gollying on the Sandgate players. But just before they could do so they were bombarded by a barrage of rotten tomatoes.

Our schoolteacher, Mr Zillman, got some of the tomato material on his jacket. He was not impressed.

I think I was the only one who had no tomato waste to deal with.

Chapter 7
MORE STORIES

Stories About Golf

I became a member of the Royal Queensland Golf Club in 1981, as a limited playing member. I had played a social round of golf with someone whilst on holidays at Noosa, and he put the idea in my mind that I should join RQ.

But the following year we had a third child. I spent considerable time and effort doing home renovations so we would have three bedrooms for children, and, for many other reasons as well, played very little golf in the years ahead. One factor, perhaps, was knee problems. I had total knee replacements in 2005 and 2006.

When I retired in 2010, I resolved to get a handicap and start playing regularly, or else cancel my membership. However, it took me two years to take action to get a handicap.

One Sunday afternoon, I went to the club to have a practice round. There I met a lady I knew (a civil engineer) and her husband. They invited me to join them in a round.

Initially I declined. 'I'd be too embarrassed,' I told them. 'I haven't been here for about five years.'

I changed my mind, however, and did join them for the round.

He was a very good golfer, with a beautiful swing. After I had played a couple of tee shots, he said to me, 'Allan, did you play a lot of cricket when you were young?'

Which, I guess, is another way of saying, 'Your backswing looks like that of a cricketer about to do a cover drive.'

Advice Ignored

On reflection, I remember a comment made by a young staff member at Main Roads many years ago. He helped organise social golf rounds for colleagues. One day he said, 'In golf, you don't *hit the ball*, you *swing the club*.'

I wish I'd understood the significance of that remark much, much earlier.

My Golf Routine

I now try to play in the competition every Wednesday. I book online and often play with people I've not played with before. When we meet on the first tee I often say, 'Look, just so you understand the context, I held a record at this club for many years.'

They usually reply by asking, 'What record was that?'

To which I respond, 'The most dollars paid per round played.'

When I first started playing in the Wednesday competitions, I used to ring up and book a place, asking to be placed in a group with others whose handicap was similar to mine. They were usually men in their late eighties. The surprising thing was that they could see where my ball went after tee shots better than I could. I guess they'd had their cataracts removed.

The Most Important Shots in Golf

I remember the day I played with an older man who shared with me some wisdom about golf. He said the two most important shots in golf are not your tee shot, but your second shot, and your first putt.

And I have to say that on the few occasions when I have had a lot of flukes in the one round and been placed among the winners, his words have proven true.

Flukes at Golf

I'm no great golfer, but it's surprising how, on some occasions, I have had a lot of flukes in the one round. On one such occasion

I was paired with a very good player in the monthly Charles Earp Jug competition, which is a four-ball, best-ball stroke event. My partner's handicap that day was twelve. Mine was thirty-two.

We had a net score of sixty-one, and we won the event. My score had counted on eleven of the eighteen holes that day. (Of course, we sometimes had the same net score, but my score was first on the card because I'd played my ball into the hole prior to him.)

When I got home and reflected on the round, I noticed that I had one-putted on five greens that day.

Par-3 Challenges

It is very rare for me to put the tee shot on the green on par-3 holes at Royal Queensland. This is especially the case with hole seventeen, which is an elevated green with a difficult, steep bunker on the right-hand side.

I went out to Golf World at Virginia some years ago and said to a person there, 'Do you ever play golf at RQ?'

'Yes,' he replied, 'I often play there.'

'Can you sell me a club that would enable me to put my tee shot on the green at the seventeenth?' I asked him.

He sold me a hybrid club with a nineteen-degree angle on the face. And, in the roughly one hundred and fifty rounds that I've used it, I've managed to put the tee shot on the green about five times.

Not long after I'd bought the club, I teed off with it at the par-3 fourth hole. I hit the ball very well. It landed on the green and was heading straight for the flag. When I got to the green, I found my ball had stopped about fifty millimetres short of the hole.

I went to get the card to record my shot for 'nearest to the pin', only to find that earlier in the round someone had had a hole in one.

Consistency

Before I play a round of golf, I like to have some practice: hit a bucket of balls, do some chipping, hit some balls out of a bunker, and have at least fifteen minutes of putting to pick up the pace of the green(s).

I practise putting with two balls. Sometimes when I putt the first ball it ends up well away from the pin. Then I hit the second ball, and it often ends up in almost the exact same spot as the first ball. It makes me think, and if anyone else has noticed I will ask, 'Am I consistent, or am I just a slow learner?'

Golf at the Royal Morocco Course in Marrakesh

In about 2012, my wife booked us on a tour of Morocco. We had a chauffeur who drove us to all the places we visited across the country.

When we were in Marrakesh, my wife wanted to have a day shopping, so she had booked me into a round of golf at the Royal Morocco course. There I had a club professional who accompanied me on the round. He drove the golf cart, set up my ball on each tee, and gave me advice about where to aim when putting, while he held the flag.

On one par-4 hole, my drive went straight down the centre of the fairway, albeit not very far. My second shot went off to the right—off the fairway, and behind some trees. I was near enough to hit a lofted shot to the green. The only trouble was that two palm trees blocked my path to the green. In the foreshortened view, the two palm trunks looked to be about six hundred millimetres apart.

As I positioned myself to make the shot, the man said to me, 'Ah … I think you should play out into the fairway.'

I ignored his advice and hit a wedge shot. It went between the tree trunks and pulled up about six hundred millimetres short of the hole.

'Tiger Woods could not have done that any better,' he said.

Learnings from Golf

Perhaps my biggest learning about golf has been the importance of taking the divot *after* the ball, not in front. But I have also learned something about human nature from taking up golf. I express it like this: 'The guy that's looking for his lost ball is always further down the fairway than the guy who finds it for him.'

My Missed Career Opportunity

One Exhibition Wednesday, I went early to RQ to have some practice before hitting off in the competition. It was a beautiful winter morning: cool but sunny, and very calm.

A lady was hitting some balls on the practice fairway. It was not common to see women golfers on the practice fairway early on a Wednesday, but this was a public holiday.

I recognised her as someone I knew, so I went over to her and I said, 'Good morning, Anne, what a beautiful morning. The only thing that could spoil today would be my golf.'

And it did.

And that is when I realised that I should have been a prophet.

More-Forgiving Roadsides

In my latter years at Main Roads, I spoke at several conferences about road safety. I was pushing the idea that we needed to put greater effort into making roadsides safer; in other words, have more-forgiving roadsides.

If you make an error whilst driving and cause a crash, perhaps you need some form of penalty, but nothing as extreme as the serious injury or death of you or your passengers. It is important for an out-of-control vehicle to be able to come to rest without a sudden impact that will cause immense harm.

I would start my speech by saying, 'Drivers are human, and humans make errors. And if you don't believe me, take up golf.'

Story from the Moscow to St Petersburg Cruise

In 2010, my wife and I took a cruise from Moscow to St Petersburg. Altogether we had ten nights onboard the ship: two in Moscow, six cruising, and two in St Petersburg.

On the final night of the cruise, the tour guides wanted to organise a concert, with performers from the tour group singing songs. At first there didn't seem to be much interest, but my wife got on the case. She got a group of Aussies to agree to perform, and also a group of English tourists, and some Texans. There were also some Israelis who were very keen to perform *Hava Nagila*.

On the morning of the day when the concert was to be held, as I was on my way to have breakfast, a young tour guide stopped me. She was endeavouring to arrange the concert programme for the evening. 'Mr Krosch,' she said, 'what songs will you Australians be singing?'

'Well, we'll have to sing "Waltzing Matilda" and perhaps "Botany Bay",' I replied.' And I added, 'Of course, if I could choose my favourite song we'd sing "Me and Bobby McGee", but we can't do that because it's an American song.'

That evening, there were about a hundred and sixty guests in the audience. There was a grand piano and a classical pianist.

The English group were first to perform. They sang 'Rule Britannia' and 'Jerusalem'.

Then we Australians were invited up and sang our two songs. We had just returned to our seats when the young tour guide I had bumped into that morning made an announcement.

'Ladies and gentlemen,' she said, 'Mr Krosch from the Australian group is going to come back up and sing "Me and Bobby McGee".'

It was a total shock to me. Fortunately, I know the lyrics off by heart, and also there was a hand-held microphone available. I assumed the pianist wouldn't have heard of the song, but perhaps she had been pre-warned because after a few bars she was providing very good accompaniment.

Watching the eyes of the audience, I concluded that my rendition went pretty well.

Next morning at breakfast two of the Texans, who were of Jewish origin, came up to me and said, 'Thank you so much for singing "Me and Bobby McGee".' One put his arm around my shoulder and, with a tear in his eye, added, 'Janis Joplin was our favourite.'

Another Story from the Russian Cruise

While on that cruise, we stopped a number of times to visit notable places. On several occasions we also had the opportunity to go to the homes of Russian families, in groups of about ten, to eat meals with them. This was so we could get to know something about Russian culture and cuisine.

When I had the opportunity to speak to Russians who spoke English, I would ask them two questions: 'What do you think of Gorbachev?' and 'What do you think of Yeltsin?' (My American co-passengers were appalled that I would ask such questions.) The answers surprised me, but they were consistent.

'Yeltsin, he was from Siberia. He was a hard, tough man. But he was a man you could trust. What he said he'd do, he did. Yes, he drank a bit too much, but so do a lot of we Russians.'

'Gorbachev? Huh. He would say whatever he thought was an appropriate comment at the time. But you couldn't trust him. And he lost the empire.'

This was quite a different view to that which I had held about Gorbachev, the man who had brought down the Iron Curtain.

A Further Story from the Russian Cruise

One day our ship was sailing down a canal when I saw a few people on shore with fishing rods. They had cast their lines into the water. I asked one of the tour guides whether they were likely to catch many fish in the canal, and if so, whether they would be good fish.

'Well, if they catch a little one they throw it back in the canal,' he replied. 'But if they catch a big one they put it in a matchbox.'

British Inventiveness

My wife and I first visited London in 1972, following my year of postgraduate study in the US. We didn't visit London again until 2004, when I made visits to all the famous museums and art galleries. The venue that most impressed me, at that stage of my life, was the Museum of Science and Industry.

You see, all countries have outstanding paintings and sculptures, but what the English did with engines in the late eighteenth century and nineteen century, in that great Industrial age, changed the world.

How Times Change

Whenever my wife and I visit London, where our eldest daughter and her family live, I like to read *The Times* newspaper.

On our visit in about 2006, a topic appeared in the newspaper, and feedback from readers was encouraged. The article postulated the following: *How can we be so prosperous, and how can it possibly last? We don't make anything anymore. Everything's made in China.*

During my time there, one Lord wrote in with his view. 'Oh, don't be so silly. Don't forget that, with regard to the item you bought in Harrods for a hundred pounds, the Chinese only got ten pounds of that. The other ninety pounds was value we added by transporting it, warehousing it, packaging it, promoting it, advertising it and selling it.'

When I was there again in 2012, *The Times* had another question: *How did we let this happen? All our skills are gone.*

Sleepwalking in Germany

There was a time when I used to work out in our swimming pool nearly every morning. Not swimming, but doing aqua-aerobics, with three styles of kicking: straight-leg kicking, lower-leg kicking, and cycling.

The neighbours in the house behind ours, adjacent to the pool, had hired an au pair, a young woman who was visiting from Germany. On several occasions I chatted to her whilst I was doing aqua-aerobics and she was putting washing on the clothesline on the other side of the pool fence.

In our first conversation she said, 'It is a wonderful place, Australia. If ever I am lost and looking at my map, someone always comes up to me and says, "Can I help you?" In Germany, no one would do that. We do not speak to strangers.'

I had a very different experience from that, and the story is a little embarrassing.

In 2011, my wife and I were extremely privileged to be part of a group of seven Brisbane people who made a tour of southern Germany and northern Austria in a ten-seater Mercedes van.

Our hosts were Emeritus Professor Miles Moody and his wife Lynne. I understand Lynne did most of the planning for the tour.

Miles and Lynne are very knowledgeable about Germany. As a young man, Miles had won a scholarship to study in Germany, and he had also spent periods of sabbatical leave there. Lynne taught German in high school, at St Margaret's, for many years. She and Miles took groups of schoolgirls on tours to Germany, every year, for much of Lynne's teaching career.

Our tour of Germany commenced in Frankfurt. My wife and I had flown into Frankfurt from Brisbane the night before the tour was to commence. I had not slept on the plane, and I had slept very little in the Frankfurt hotel.

In the morning, we were picked up in the Mercedes and introduced to the other members of the party.

We were in a wine-growing area, and we spent the day visiting historic places and some wineries, where we did some wine tasting.

In the late afternoon we came to a small, historic town called Freinsheim. Freinsheim still has the barrier wall around the centre of the town that was built to protect the town from invaders. I understand it is the only town in Germany that still has the entire wall of this type.

In the late afternoon, we climbed up to the level of the wall from which soldiers had fired their arrows (or bullets) at advancing invaders through the gaps in the top of the wall.

We then checked into a small hotel. Miles had some difficulty manoeuvring the Mercedes from the narrow laneway into the parking area of the hotel. The other members of our group were allocated rooms in the upstairs level, but my wife and I were assigned a room at ground level, with a doorway to the car park.

We all went out to a restaurant, where we had a fine German dinner and some glasses of local wine. Then it was time to get some sleep.

Because I'd had very little sleep the previous two nights, I thought I'd better take a sleeping tablet. I had brought some with me, a type I'd never taken before called Stillnox.

I got off to sleep quickly, and during the night I had an intense dream. In my dream, I was crawling along the ground adjacent to some walls (my dream was undoubtedly influenced by our visit to the city defence wall in the late afternoon).

Then suddenly I was awake—and walking along a street. I realised I had been sleepwalking, but I had no idea for how long. It was obviously late because there was very little activity about. It was fairly cold, and I was walking barefoot on a cobblestone road. The worst thing was that I was wearing a pyjama top only; no pyjama pants (I never wear pyjama pants as I find them uncomfortable when lying in bed).

So I found myself in that state, and I didn't know where I was. I didn't know where we were staying, either. I was afraid that when the morning came and I was still in that state of undress, the police would be called and I'd be taken into custody.

Suddenly a car came by and stopped. A window went down and the lone female driver said, in accented English: 'Are you okay?'

'No,' I replied. 'I've been sleepwalking. I don't know where I am, and I don't know what hotel I'm staying in.'

'Get in,' she said. 'I'll drive you to my home and my husband can help you.'

'Have you got something I can put around me?' I said.

She gave me an old blanket and put her little dog in the back seat. I sat in the front passenger seat and she drove me to her home. Then her husband came and set out to drive me to various small hotels to see if I could recognise the one where I was staying.

At the second one, by chance, I recognised the car-park entrance where Miles had experienced difficulty getting the ten-seater vehicle through the driveway. Had he not had that issue, I would have had no chance of identifying where we were staying.

So I was safely home. The door to our hired room was unlocked, and my wife was safe and asleep.

At breakfast the next morning I decided to share my experience with the other members of the group. I chose to do so as a result of something I had learned at a course on experiential leadership development, which I had attended some twelve years earlier. The concept was that the sharing of feelings helps to build teamwork.

I'm not altogether sure it was wise of me to tell the story, because I got a bit of ribbing as a result.

After breakfast, we went out on tour and visited further places of interest and more wineries.

When we arrived back at the hotel in the late afternoon, there was a package that had been delivered for me. Inside was a small, framed oil painting—the work of the man who had assisted me the night before. He had hand-delivered it to the hotel, together with an envelope containing a card with a written message: *I am an artist, and since I was able to assist you last night, perhaps when you get back to Australia you could help me by endeavouring to find an art dealer who would be willing to offer my works for sale.*

He had provided his postal address.

I wanted to meet him and his wife again, to express my great thanks for the assistance they had given me. However, we had a dining commitment that evening, and an early start the next morning so I didn't have the opportunity to do so.

When I got back to Australia, I made contact with two ladies associated with artwork. One is a painter herself and operates a private art gallery. The other was a former art teacher. Both advised me that I would have no prospect of finding a gallery owner who would be willing to sell the German artist's work.

So I had a dilemma. I wanted to express my enormous thanks and gratitude to the man and his wife for their assistance, but it seemed I couldn't do it in the way he had sought. I thought of sending cash, but I didn't want to cause offence by sending an amount that they considered insufficient.

I decided to write a letter to express my gratitude. I also made the offer that if ever they visited Australia, we would be delighted to provide them accommodation in our home, and to be their tour guide to Brisbane.

I also included a copy of the Henry Lawson poem 'The Fire on Ross's Farm', which I felt, and still feel, expresses very well the Australian spirit of helping others in trouble.

However, I never received a response.

Story of an Ungiven Speech

One Saturday morning in about 1980, I was with one of my tennis colleagues when he bid, successfully, for a prestige heritage home in Hendra. Built in the late 1880s, the house had a tennis court, and I played there with our tennis group for a few years before my knees put an end to my tennis.

When the home was a hundred years old, my friend held a centenary party, to which my wife and I were invited. It was a splendid occasion. A few men came dressed in top hats and tails, and their wives also wore attire that mirrored the era. Some came driving antique cars.

My friend, the host, had asked me to make a speech at the event. I duly prepared a speech, but on the night he had so many other speakers that I was never called upon to deliver it. If I had, this is what I would have said:

'Brisbane became a convict settlement in 1824. German missionaries came to Nundah in 1838. The first other free settlers came in 1842. So, in just over forty years, Brisbane changed from a new settlement to a town where a mansion-building era took place. Some of the mansions from that era were designed by an architect of Italian origin named Andrea Stombuco. Brisbane did not have another mansion-building era until the 1980s.

I wonder how Brisbane had become prosperous enough to have a mansion-building era in the 1880s. Of course, Brisbane and Queensland were part of a great empire: the British Empire. That would have been a factor, offering markets for products like wool. But probably the real explanation was the discovery of gold. Though gold was not discovered near Brisbane, it was discovered in Gympie and other places in Queensland.

I understand that Melbourne, in the 1880s, was one of the wealthiest cities in the world on a wealth-per-head-of-population basis. This had followed from the discoveries of gold at Ballarat and Bendigo.

Of course, booms don't last forever. For instance, the boom of the 1880s was followed by a period of depression in the 1890s. But certainly the 1880s would have been a great era in Brisbane, and it has left us with many architectural treasures.'

Another Story About Anniversaries

A year of some significance in the Ascot–Hamilton area must have been 1920. Two entities celebrated their centenaries in 2020: the

Royal Queensland Golf Club and Ascot State School.

Each of my three children attended Ascot State School. I was not a student there, but I did serve on the parents and citizens committee for quite a few years, including a term as president.

So when I was informed, in 2019, that an information meeting was to be held in the school hall to advise attendees about planning for the centenary event, I decided to attend.

We were informed that former students would be encouraged to submit brief memoirs of their time at Ascot State School, and that these would provide the contents of a book to be published.

When my daughter in London had prepared her memoir, she emailed it to me with a message: *Dad, can you edit it for me and submit it? I am so busy here, organising an event at the school where my boys go—Dulwich College. There are 1200 people coming to the event, which is for the school's 400th anniversary.*

Centenary of 26 Ascot Street

In 1908, an eminent legal family called Macnish built a large house in Ascot Street. The home was named Brentwood. Two years later, they built a house next door for their daughter. That one was named Ardgur. And that is the house that my wife and I have owned since late 1974.

I understand that both houses were designed by a famous architect named Robin Dods.

Our house was built on a parcel of land that is now occupied by four houses. Along part of the Ascot Street frontage there was a tennis court. In the rear were stables for horses, which were needed in the pre-automobile era.

I understand that somewhere in the 1950s Brentwood burned down. The land was subdivided, and six homes were built: three facing Ascot Street and three facing Ormond Street. Two of those facing Ascot Street have recently been demolished and replaced by one large house.

When our house was approaching its centenary, I had the idea to hold a centenary party. However, my wife was not cooperative. She thought it was silly to have a party for a house.

I made some effort to research the history of the house, and found out about an architect called Robert Riddell, who had written a book about the works of Robin Dods. I invited him to visit and inspect the house, which he did.

I planned to have a centenary dinner party in our main dining room, with just twelve people present: my wife and I, Robert Riddell and his partner; and four couples who had lived in our street when we first moved in, and whom we had got to know well. I found a caterer who was willing to come and prepare the meal in our kitchen.

Unfortunately, for a number of reasons the event did not take place. Robert Riddell was not available on the date that I had first chosen due, if I recall correctly, to an absence from Brisbane. My wife's negative attitude may also have been a factor.

I regret not holding the event. One of my learnings from life is the importance of marking the milestones along life's journey.

Story About Doughnut Making at the Ascot School Fete

During my time on the Ascot State School parents and citizens committee, fetes were held periodically to raise revenue for committee initiatives. At one fete, I accepted the responsibility of being the organiser of a doughnut stall.

I arranged with Defiance Flour, then operating at Albion, to hire a doughnut-making cooker, and sourced the cooking oil and ingredients to make the doughnuts.

We were provided with a stall—a small tent with a front counter—and the equipment we needed, including an electric-power lead.

We were in an outdoor area that was busy with people, and our doughnuts were very much in demand. We couldn't make them fast enough.

The doughnut maker, square in shape and filled with hot oil, had provision for nine doughnuts to be cooked in each batch. There was a submerged grille, with a handle, that was used to lift the doughnuts out when they were cooked. The raw doughnut mixture was dispensed into the hot oil using a purpose-built implement. The doughnuts were dispensed in a 3x3 pattern, and the nine doughnuts came out circular, each with a circular hole in the centre.

I had several people helping out on the stall. One man, who was from our tennis group, had had great success as a property developer. To increase the rate of doughnut production, he insisted on dispensing the mixture in a 4x4 pattern to make sixteen doughnuts in each batch, not nine.

I was initially averse to this idea. Being a bit of a perfectionist, I felt that a doughnut should be circular in shape, with a circular hole in the middle. Now they were emerging square-ish in shape, with a smaller central hole.

I had to turn up the heat a bit to cook sixteen in the same time it had been taking to cook a batch of nine. Though the doughnuts didn't look as good, they still tasted just as good. However, the rate of production was still less than needed to meet the demand.

Then my 'head chef' decided to dispense the pre-mixed doughnut batter in a 5x5 pattern. This required very speedy and accurate dispensing. The temperature had to be turned up a bit more to ensure that the cooking time did not increase.

Now the doughnuts had no central hole at all, and were entirely square and much thicker. But they still tasted good and were just as sought after by customers.

So my friend had effectively increased the rate of doughnut production from nine per batch to twenty-five per batch, an increase of nearly three hundred percent.

No wonder he had done well in business.

Guarding Paintings in the Ascot School Hall

During my term as president of the committee at Ascot State School, the committee organised an art exhibition/sale as a fundraising event.

Artists, art dealers and parents who had paintings they wished to sell all had an opportunity to hang paintings in the school hall early on a Saturday morning. The exhibition opened at midday and closed late Saturday evening. Unsold paintings were taken away on Sunday. This meant that the unsold paintings hung in the hall overnight.

It would have been too costly for the committee to arrange insurance cover for the event, so two fathers of school students were asked to stay in the hall overnight to ensure no paintings were stolen. One of those fathers was myself, and the other was George Hood, a man I had got to know well when he did plumbing work at our home.

On Saturday night, after the exhibition closed, George and I laid out our sleeping bags on the upper-level section of seating at the rear of the hall. George had brought a baseball bat as a weapon to use against any intruders.

We both fell asleep at about midnight. Some hours later we were abruptly awoken by a crashing sound below us, in the hall. We sprang to our feet. I quickly turned on the lights. George grabbed his baseball bat and we rushed down to confront the intruders.

We didn't find any intruders. What had happened was that one large painting had fallen off the wall and hit the floor. Either the supporting wire had broken, or the hook to which it was attached had failed. Fortunately, the fallen painting and frame had incurred no damage.

We went back up to our sleeping spots, but I don't think I got any further sleep that night.

Chapter 8

HUMAN NATURE

Story of My Speech to a Group of Young Engineers

About a year after I had retired, I was approached by someone from Engineers Australia and asked if I would be willing to give a speech to a group of young engineers. I was asked to reflect on my own career and perhaps provide the attendees with a few tips, or guidance, on shaping their own careers.

I put a lot of thought into the content of my address. I started my speech like this (trying to sound grave): 'Ladies and gentlemen, I am old enough to have some wisdom, and at this stage of my life there are three ideas that come frequently to my mind. One, it's funny how life turns out. Two, it's marvellous what webs interconnect people. And three, it's funny how little things can have a big effect.'

I didn't give them any actual examples, but let me share with you now an example of each one of those three ideas.

It's Funny How Life Turns Out

In primary school I had always been first or second in class. When I started high school, I elected to take subjects relevant to my becoming an architect. That had been my father's suggestion.

Down on the farm, my sister (two years older than me), my brother (two years younger than me) and I shared the task of washing the dishes after meals. The three phases—washing up, wiping up and putting away—were rotated weekly so the tasks were shared equally between the three of us.

When it was my turn to dry the dishes with a tea towel, I would stack them vertically to make towers. It was that tendency that led my father to the idea of me becoming an architect.

(Forgive me for this digression, but I should add that for breakfast I had porridge two weeks out of three. In the weeks when I was doing the washing up, I elected to have cornflakes instead. My siblings never made any mention of this.)

After I finished grade ten at high school, I changed my career plan and decided to study subjects with a view to becoming a civil engineer. I had the idea that I could be the designer of great bridges, like Sir John Bradfield, who was the chief engineer for both the Sydney Harbour Bridge and the Story Bridge in Brisbane.

At the end of grade twelve, I was dux of my school (Banyo State High School) and won the prize for English. The vocational guidance officer advised me to become a lawyer or a writer, but I ignored that advice. Instead, I took a Main Roads scholarship to study at the University of Queensland and become a civil engineer.

So, it's funny how life turns out.

(Another digression. After graduating, I worked in road construction. Then, after a few years, I was supported to do a master's degree at Purdue University in Indiana, USA. On my return, I worked as a project manager on freeway design, in the first freeway-building era in Brisbane. After Prime Minister Gough Whitlam took away the money for urban freeways, I shifted into the field of planning—not project planning, but planning studies for road networks in cities and in the country. Thereafter I had roles in management of various areas dealing with policy, strategy and traffic operations. In those roles, I spent a fair bit of time putting words on paper anyway.)

The Webs That Interconnect People

Many years ago, my wife and I were invited to attend the Dalby Picnic Races. We attended for a number of years. We were billeted by friends of friends, and we got to know them well. We also became well acquainted with a couple who were relatives of our hosts.

Quite some years ago, the couple who were relatives of our hosts, sold their property in the country and came to live in Brisbane. We would meet up with them socially from time to time, and still do.

They invited us to the christening of a grandchild, to be held one Saturday morning at the Enoggera Army Barracks chapel.

(Their daughter had married a man who was in the army).

Following the christening, we went to our friends' home for lunch. There the godfather, who was also in the army, introduced himself to me. His surname was the same as a cousin of my mother, who had come from Bundaberg. I asked the man if he came from Bundaberg.

He seemed somewhat taken aback. 'Well, I come from near Bundaberg,' he said. 'Why would you ask that?'

I said, 'You see, on that side of my family my great-grandfather, as a child, was in the very first group of Europeans who settled in Bundaberg. His name was Abraham Pegg.'

A smile crossed the man's face, and he extended his hand. As we shook hands he said, 'We share the same great-grandfather.'

It's marvellous what webs interconnect people.

Little Things Can Have a Big Effect

I was twenty-two years old and going to Queensland University to play a game of rugby league one Saturday afternoon when my mother asked me to drop off something to my father, who was at a church working-bee.

When I pulled up outside the church, I saw a friend of Dad's and asked him if he would give the package to Dad.

'Where are you going?' he asked me.

'I'm going out to uni to play rugby league,' I replied.

'Give it up,' he said, 'before you hurt yourself.'

I ignored that advice.

I played front row forward. During the game, I made a big break downfield. All I needed to do was pass to my winger; he would run forward, commit their winger and pass the ball back to me as I ran behind him, and I'd score in the corner.

But when he got the ball, he thought he was a halfback. He didn't run forward as I'd expected; instead he sidestepped on the spot.

I was about to collide with my own teammate. I felt a force come on my left leg as I endeavoured to avoid a collision, and I hadn't had enough time to tense my muscles around the knee to protect the joint. My knee was wobbly. Without a hand being laid on me, I'd ruptured the posterior cruciate ligament.

After that, I could walk and even jog, but I could never sprint again.

I sought advice from a top knee surgeon in Sydney. He said that if it were an anterior cruciate ligament, he would operate. And if I were a professional footballer, he would operate on my posterior cruciate ligament. But for me, he recommended no surgery.

I continued to play tennis but had to give it up in my mid-thirties.

Because I pushed myself too hard at work, I had to exercise regularly to sleep better. For about fifteen years after I came to live in Ascot, I jogged each morning for about fifteen minutes on the Ascot State School oval. When I couldn't jog anymore, I walked every morning for about ten more years—down Crescent Road, along Kingsford Smith Drive, and back up Gray's Road.

Over the years I had two operations, on each of my knees, to trim up the meniscus damage. Eventually I was bone-into-bone and had to have total knee replacements.

The damage to my right knee had occurred when I was on holiday at Noosa, walking down a set of concrete steps to clean some fish I had caught. I wasn't watching where I was going, and didn't realise how much the tidewater had washed away the sand at the bottom, leaving a much higher step than previously. As the force came on my right leg, the knee tried to flex in the reverse direction and I cracked the meniscus, the tissue that separates the knee bones.

I once asked my orthopaedic specialist when biotechnology was going to save me.

'It's coming,' he answered, 'but it will be too late for you.'

So these are two instances where little things had a big effect.

Story from Nevada, USA

Towards the end of my period of study at Purdue University, Indiana, the first Earth Summit was held in Rio de Janeiro in 1972. It got a lot of coverage in the US media.

The message was all about the fragility of Earth and the environment, and about what changes mankind needed to make.

Some months later, my wife and I were travelling cross the

United States by car. I had a series of meetings with officers of Road Authorities in a number of different places in the US and Canada. I had driven north from Lafayette, Indiana for meetings in Toronto, then southwest to Kansas, south through Oklahoma, and down to Texas. (May I mention, in passing, that one of the places I most enjoyed visiting in the US was the Cowboy Hall of Fame in Oklahoma City.)

After my meetings in Texas, we headed up to California via Nevada. When entering Nevada, we drove past the Hoover Dam, and stopped to read some of the messages on the monuments.

The Hoover Dam was built in the Depression years, to help create employment. A monument we viewed, with an epitaph dated 1932, had been built in memory of those brave men who had given their lives in their effort to conquer nature during the building of the dam.

I stood looking at the monument and thought how much change had occurred during that forty-year period with regard to how mankind viewed planet Earth; how nature had shifted from being harsh and difficult to conquer, to being something that was fragile and needed care and attention.

Forty years is a short time in the history of this planet, and in the period of mankind's occupation of it. But humans are creatures of habit, and it takes a significant shock to cause a change of habits.

In my next story I have more to say on this topic.

Humans Are Creatures of Habit

My wife and I had been on an overseas holiday, which ended with a period of time spent in London with our eldest daughter and her family. Our daughter was about to have her second child, so her mother remained behind to provide support and I travelled home alone.

I arrived back in Brisbane on a Friday morning. I went to get the mail from a neighbour, who had kindly collected it in our absence. There was a large amount of mail, and I put it aside to read later. My first priority was maintenance of the lawn, gardens and swimming pool.

In the evening, I went to my office to deal with all the mail, but when I went to turn on the light in the office all the lights in the house went off.

I managed to find a torch and went down to the switchboard, where I found one of the circuit breakers had been tripped. I tried to push it back into its normal position, but I couldn't do so until after I had gone back upstairs to my office and turned off the light switch.

The next morning I tried to find out what was causing the problem, to see if it was something I could fix. I soon realised that I would need to get an electrician to come and deal with the problem. I decided to let that wait until Monday morning. I had a lot of issues to deal with, and it would cost less for the electrician to come on a weekday rather than the weekend.

So I knew that when I went to my office I shouldn't turn on the light switch because it would trip the circuit breaker again. But over the course of that weekend, how many times do you think I walked into my office, flipped the light switch and tripped the circuit breaker, even though I knew not to do so.

I think it was about six times—until I got some sticky tape and placed it over the switch to prevent me from doing it again.

That experience made me realise the extent to which we humans are creatures of habit. Many of the things we do are pure reflex action, done without conscious thought. And to get us to change our habits requires a fairly big 'shock'.

Human Affairs and Their Complexity

I once read that it is in the nature of human affairs to become more complex with time, but throughout history there have been great crises—for example, wars and depressions—that have cleaned out all the complications and made things simpler again—for a while.

But in Australia we haven't had a major event like this for a long time, and a huge amount of complexity and complication has built up in this country.

As an example of how a crisis can eliminate complications, I'd like to tell the story of the Inland Defence Road. When the Japanese military forces were heading towards Australia in 1942, there was a decision to build the Inland Defence Road, which could not be bombed by planes from Japanese aircraft carriers. It ran from Ipswich to Charters Towers via Duaringa.

The road was earth formed and gravel paved, but not bitumen sealed. There were many bridges, some of them high and long, and all were built of timber. Altogether, the road that was built was 1411 kilometres long. This was all constructed in about nine months.

Today, it would probably take that long to get a decision on the brief to be used to engage the consulting firm to carry out the environmental-impact study.

Another example is the construction of the aircraft landing strip at Charters Towers. Main Roads crews were assembled to build the landing strip; it was from there that the American military aircraft flew to bomb the Japanese naval fleet in the battle of the Coral Sea.

When the first group of American aircraft arrived at Charters Towers, they had to circle above for a time until compaction of the landing-strip pavement was completed.

Thoughts While Circling Over Sydney in an Aeroplane

I was on a flight to Sydney one time, and there was a significant delay before the plane could land. It circled over Sydney for quite some time. From my window seat, I looked out at all the buildings in that city.

I thought about the huge amount of human effort that would have been involved in building just one of them, and there were so many of them.

And I thought about how you could go into any one of those buildings, and in every room you could turn on a switch and a light would come on.

You could go into another room, turn on a tap, and drinkable water would flow out.

You could go into another room, press a button, and the water there would flow away to be treated elsewhere.

And it all works very well, nearly all of the time.

And I thought: *What a remarkable species mankind is.*

A Thought Whilst on the Roof of a Block of Units

I am the chairman of the body-corporate committee of a block of units in Clayfield. A few years ago, when the age of digital television arrived, we had to get new TV aerials installed on the roof of the building.

I was present when the technician was up on the roof installing the new aerials.

He called out to me: 'I think you should climb up the ladder and have a look at this roof.'

There was significant rusting of the galvanised-metal roof sheeting, and we had to have new roof sheeting installed.

Whilst I was up on the roof, I looked towards the southwest, where the television transmission towers are located on Mt Coot-tha. I thought about how television content is conveyed from those towers through the sky to the aerials on the roof, and then finds its way to the television screens in the units.

And I thought: *Mankind is a remarkable form of life to have made the discoveries that enable such a process to take place.*

Optimising Efficiency of Supermarket Shopping

Earlier I told the story of how my wife had to have an operation to remove a benign meningioma on the edge of her brain. After she'd had that surgery, I had to do the supermarket shopping for some months. To make shopping efficient, I always prepared a list of items to be purchased. I then went a step further.

Whilst at Coles, I noted down the number of the aisle where each of the items on my list was located. I then ordered my list by aisle number.

My younger daughter, who was always my little helper, accompanied me when I did the shopping.

I had a further idea to improve shopping efficiency. Instead of pushing the trolley up and down all the relevant aisles, I would push the trolley along the end of all the aisles and despatch my daughter to run down each relevant aisle, telling her what to get.

That reduced the time of my shopping trips enormously.

Chapter 9

STORIES FROM MY MAIN ROADS DAYS

My Charles Barton Story

When I was awarded a Main Roads scholarship to study at university in 1964, the commissioner of Main Roads was Charlie Barton (later Sir Charles Barton). He was appointed commissioner following the change of government after some forty years of a Labor government.

As a young man, he had worked in the Bridge Branch at Main Roads. In World War II he served in North Africa, and was made a prisoner of war by the Germans. After the war, he worked in an engineering consulting firm in Mackay.

He was a tall, dignified man who spoke slowly. He was a man of few words.

He decentralised Main Roads and created thirteen districts across Queensland. He assigned a professionally qualified civil engineer to serve as District Engineer in each of the districts.

He called all the District Engineers together to address them before they were dispatched to take up their new roles. I was not present when he made this speech because I was still at university, but I heard recounts of it several times. My understanding is that it would have gone something like this:

'I'm putting you out there to live and work in your community. I'm putting you there to know your road system firsthand; and I'm putting you there to know your community's needs firsthand. And I'm putting you there to make decisions. And I want you to make the decision. Mind you, I want you to think about it before you make it, and as long as you do that, I'll back you even if things go bad.

If we do that, we'll be a good department, but if we want to be a *great* department, we'll need one other thing. We'll need, in our headquarters, experts in various fields who are keeping up to date with world's best practice, and feeding that information through to you and your practitioners, who'll be too busy day to day with your work to be keeping up with all of that. And if we do those two things, we'll be a great department.'

More About Charles Barton

In April 1968, the group of Main Roads scholarship holders who had come to Brisbane for the University graduation ceremony had attended a meeting at Main Roads, where Charles Barton addressed us.

The little thing that sticks in my mind is hearing him say that if ever we were down in Brisbane we should pay a visit to his office and say hello. And if he was not present, we should sign the visitor's book so he would know we'd called in.

It was a significant statement because it told our group of young engineers that we were important to him.

My Russ Hinze Story

When I was a young man, the minister for Main Roads was Russ Hinze. (He later had local government and racing added to his portfolio, and came to be called the Minister for Everything.)

Russ Hinze once gave a lunchtime speech at Blackwater. In the speech, he said that he was going to build a new road north from Blackwater, across the Bedford Weir. That pleased the locals, but not the Broadsound Shire Council, which wanted a new road on a different route. They arranged for a deputation to the minister.

At that time, as a young engineer I had some responsibility for the planning of roads to serve the new coalmining towns in the Bowen Basin. I was given the task of writing the briefing note for the minister, for him to use in his meeting with the council representatives.

On the day of the deputation, I accompanied the Main Roads commissioner, Mr Bill Hansen, to brief the minister prior to the representatives arriving, and then attend the meeting with him.

When we got to the minister's office, we found that the deputation had arrived early, and the minister had already joined them in his conference room. We had no opportunity to brief him in advance.

The deputation consisted of the mayor of the Broadsound Shire, the shire clerk (now termed CEO), the shire engineer, and the local member of parliament. The local member stood up and started the conversation by outlining the situation.

The minister was focused on reading the briefing note I had prepared. He had it tucked under the table near his waist.

Then a telephone on the table adjacent to the minister's left arm rang. He picked it up and began speaking quietly. The local member continued making his remarks.

The minister hung up the phone and resumed reading the briefing note. The local member kept speaking.

Then the phone rang a second time, and the minister took the call. That brought everything to a halt.

When the minister hung up for the second time, Mr Hansen tried to bring some order to the proceedings. 'Mr Minister,' he said, 'I think what the shire is trying to say is—'

The minister slammed his fist down on the table and said loudly, 'Don't tell me what the shire is trying to say. I know exactly what they're trying to say. I think they're just plain bloody jealous, and quite frankly they give me the shits.'

I don't know how the meeting kept going, but somehow it did.

The minister asked the shire representatives when they were going to relocate their headquarters from the coast to one of the new mining towns. This led to further discussion on a number of topics. The meeting then came to an end, and the shire representatives left in what seemed a reasonably favourable state of mind.

As Mr Hansen and I were getting into the elevator to depart, he said to me, 'Well, Allan, what did you make of that?'

'Mr Hansen,' I replied, 'I think I've got a story for my memoirs.'

'Have you really?' he said. 'It wouldn't rate a mention in mine.'

Story About Organisational Identity

In 1974, the Federal Government declared a set of roads to be national highways, which would be funded federally. The Bruce Highway was one of them.

They applied very high standards of flood immunity to these highways, planning for them to be built one metre above maximum known flood levels. This would have involved a lot of money on national highways in some parts of Northern Queensland.

As a young engineer involved in road network planning, I had the idea that if we had better information about road outage due to flooding, we might be able to save money. We could perhaps avoid the great expense of building some roads to a higher level if we could divert traffic to other parts of the network when those sections of national highways were closed due to flooding.

However, we had virtually no information available about road closure due to flooding, and, in particular, no information about concurrent closure. I searched other possible sources of information, such as the weather bureau, but I could find nothing of value.

A meeting of senior Main Roads officers from across the State was to be convened shortly. I arranged to be given an opportunity to speak to them about this matter.

On the day of the meeting, I started by saying, 'Next wet season, I'd like you to have an officer, on each day, get a district map and colour in any sections of road closed due to flooding. And then send those maps down to me. That will enable me, over time, to build up a picture of road outages due to flooding, and particularly of concurrent outages.'

The divisional engineer from Townsville sprang to his feet. 'Mr Chairman,' he said, 'this is not Main Roads' role. We only provide the roads; we don't operate them.'

And in many respects that comment was correct. In the countryside, there was often a railway line running parallel to the road. If there was a derailment, Queensland Rail had to deal with it. If there was a crash on the road, the ambulance, tow trucks and police showed up—but not Main Roads officers. If a fatality had occurred, Main Roads and Police Department personnel would meet on site later to see if there were any contributing road factors.

However, in a just-in-time world, it is important that the

road authority takes appropriate responsibility for road-incident management. That involved a change of organisational self-concept, or identity. That would mean a change within the road authority, to see itself as not only road planner, road designer, road constructor and road maintainer – but also as road-network operator.

In my latter career, I endeavoured to have Main Roads embrace the concept of road-system operator as part of its identity. I came to believe that identity is a very important concept for organisations. They all have strategic plans that spell out their mission, vision and values, but few, at least whilst I was working, expressly included the concept of identity.

This reminds me of something I once read in a book by Lawrie Lawrence, the famous Australian Olympic swimming coach. If I remember correctly, he said that he never knew of a swimmer who'd won an Olympic gold medal who, as a young person, had not closed their eyes before getting into bed every night and visualised themselves in an Olympic-medal presentation ceremony.

My Chief Engineer Story

When I came down to Brisbane in April 1968 to attend our graduation ceremony, I was required to attend a meeting with the chief engineer. He was a man approaching sixty-five years of age, which was the age of retirement.

I was approaching his office on floor seven of the Spring Hill building at the scheduled time of ten-thirty am when I noticed that a lady with a tea trolley had just departed his office and was heading down the corridor.

The door to his office was open. I saw him staring at the cup of tea on the desk in front of him. I knocked on his office wall, but he didn't seem to hear me. I knocked again, more loudly.

He looked up and saw me. 'Oh, come in', he said. 'I was just deciding whether to have one lump or two.'

On reflection, it seems to me that in those days, men of sixty-five appeared to be much older than they do today. We had a commissioner named Harry Lowe. He retired at sixty-five and, sadly, didn't reach sixty-six. He was succeeded by Commissioner Bill Hansen, who retired at sixty-two and didn't make sixty-three.

The advances in health care have greatly benefitted the baby-boomer generation, and the generations following.

Story About the Story Bridge

In early 1988, my boss gave me a task: to prepare a paper on the traffic planning for the Story Bridge and present it at an Engineers Australia event. In the bicentenary year of 1988, the Story Bridge was approaching its fiftieth anniversary. Engineers Australia held an event to honour the bridge and those who created it.

In preparing that paper, I had the assistance of a young engineer named Adam Pekol. Our paper was one of three presented at the event. One was about the structural design of the bridge, and another was about the construction.

My boss had obtained all the files about the planning for the Story Bridge from the archives of the Main Roads Commission/Main Roads Department. I spent many hours over the hot nights of January reading through them. There was a lot of interesting content, like how few digits there were in a Brisbane telephone number in the 1920s.

The chief engineer for the Story Bridge was Dr John Bradfield. He had been the chief engineer for design and construction of the Sydney Harbour Bridge.

I would like to share with you some of the things Dr Bradfield said at the sod-turning ceremony, at the commencement of construction. These remarks were reported in the *Telegraph* newspaper.

He said: 'It is said that we are living in a cold engineering age from which romance has fled. But there is more romance and action in the world today than ever before: you just need to have the eyes to see and the ears to hear to appreciate and understand.'

He said he had 'endeavoured, in designing the bridge, to demonstrate the artistry and poetry of the science of engineering; so as to express in the bridge simplicity, beauty and service'.

He spoke about how many tons of concrete would be used in the foundations of the bridge, and how many tons of steel would be used in the structure of the bridge. And he mentioned that the hand railings would be a warm grey colour because the concrete would contain granite and jasper, which had to be brought from the Gympie district.

He said that the only other place he knew of where jasper had been used in construction was in the walls of the New Jerusalem, which is mentioned in the Bible in the book of Revelations.

He continued: 'So, if you think I am making the Brisbane Bridge too soon, just picture the city Brisbane must become. As the state flourishes and becomes more populated, so Brisbane will respond and pulsate with new life and vigour. Its population will reach the million mark in less than fifty years, and two million well within a hundred years from now, a beautiful city, semi-circular and diademed with hills, some day to rank as the second city of the Commonwealth. The cantilever bridge with its bold towers and curved outline, sturdy shoulders, with graceful curves, will harmonise with the picturesque and rugged beauty of the Brisbane skyline.'

And to the children he said: 'As you see the bridge grow day by day, you will be proud of all those who are building it, and when you become men and women I know you will strive to follow their example and work together for the good of our beautiful country.'

Story About the Gateway Project

I was once a member of a committee of senior officers who were responsible for oversight of a project called the 'Gateway

Project'. (This was a computer system development project and had nothing at all to do with the Gateway Bridges.)

A lot of effort had been expended in the planning phase of the project. Then, prior to a decision being made to proceed to the development phase, a risk-management workshop was conducted.

At the outset, there was a lot of confidence about the soundness of the project. But somehow, during the discussions a seed of doubt emerged, and it escalated to the point that some thought the project should not proceed.

The person facilitating the workshop turned to me and said, 'Allan, what do you think?'

I instantly replied: 'Any man, having put his hand to the plough, and looking back, is not fit for the kingdom of heaven.' (A little thing that must have stuck in my mind from church attendance as a child.)

So the project proceeded, albeit with a significant degree of cost overrun, if I recall correctly.

Chapter 10

LEARNINGS

To Know But Not To Do

I think the biggest learning in my life is expressed in the phrase: 'To know but not to do is not yet to know.' That is, the world pays you for what you do, not for what you know to do (but don't get around to doing).

Looking back on my life, I can see that I had a good ability to foresee the future, and to know what to do, but I let myself down by not doing what I knew to do.

Let me give an example.

My wife and I had managed, over time, to obtain ownership of several investment properties, commercial and industrial. In the early 1990s, I resolved that we should make one more major property purchase and have the loan paid off by the time I retired. But in the early 1990s inflation was high and interest rates went to very high levels, so I postponed any action.

Then in 1996 there was a change in the Queensland State Government, and I got into a very demanding role at Main Roads. Suddenly it was the early 2000s. A decade had gone by and I had done nothing about that further commercial property acquisition.

I got a real estate agent on the case and he identified a property for sale in Campbell Street, Bowen Hills. Based on what he told me, I decided we should buy it. When he brought me the lease and I'd studied it, I realised the investment proposition was not quite as good as I'd first been led to believe, but it was still a worthy investment.

The agent offered to meet me on site for an inspection of the property. I asked my wife to come with me, since she would be a co-owner. Had I not taken her there, I would certainly have proceeded with the purchase.

On the day of the inspection, I drove home at lunchtime to pick up my wife and we met the agent on site. We inspected the interior of the building and walked around the exterior.

My wife said to the agent, 'What's this place next door with all the towels on the line?'

He had a wry smile on his face as he said, 'It's, um, a house of ill repute.'

To make light of the issue, I said, 'Perhaps we should be buying the property next door. It might provide a higher return on investment.'

I drove my wife home and went back to work. In the evening on my way home from work, I stopped near the building we had inspected earlier that day with the intention of purchasing. I saw taxis pulling up outside the adjacent property, and the thought came into my mind: *How can I, having been raised in the Methodist religion, purchase a property next door to a brothel?*

So I pulled out of the deal. And we never did get around to making that one further major purchase of an investment property.

The irony was that some months later, the property next door was no longer operating as a house of ill repute, and the property I decided not to purchase has been occupied ever since by a very successful company. Furthermore, the town-planning laws were changed, and now, adjacent to that site, there are twenty-storey apartment buildings.

Never Read a Speech

In the period from 1988 to 1992, Main Roads set up a change-management project called Road Reform. It was about the change to embrace the principles of commercialisation and competition that had followed the moves of Thatcher and Reagan towards the ideology of free markets and a lesser role for government organisations. (In the years prior to this, Main Roads expenditure on road construction had been apportioned approximately a third each to Main Roads day-labour crews, local government workforces, and road contractors in the private sector.)

I was a member of the Road Reform project team. Towards the end of the project, I was called upon to make a speech about the outcome of the project at a gathering of representatives from local governments in the central–western areas of Queensland. The event was held in Capella. There was the intention of having a similar speech made to gatherings of local governments in other regions of Queensland also.

My speech ended just prior to lunch being served. From watching the eyes of members of the audience, I felt the speech had been very successful and had been well received so I sat down to lunch feeling very happy.

I should make it clear that I never read a speech to an audience. In preparing a speech, I mind-map my ideas and write out the text of my speech. Then I distil the key points and prepare a set of palm cards with brief notes to give myself a reminder should that be necessary.

I had nearly finished my lunch when a secretary came up to see me.

'Because a speech similar to yours will be made by other speakers in other regions, Mr Krosch,' she said, 'I was asked to record your speech. I have just finished typing up what you presented. Could I get you to run your eye over it, please, and let me know if you'd like me to make any changes?'

When I read what she had typed, I was initially appalled. How could I, who was so experienced in writing reports and submissions, speak like that: those long rambling sentences and repetitive phrases?

But that's when I realised that we don't speak to each other in the way we write to each other. If we watch the eyes of the audience, we notice if some have failed to take in the point made, and that will cause us to say it again, or in a slightly different way to ensure that our message has been correctly received; hence the amount of repetition.

That is to say, there is an interaction between speaker and audience: verbal and non-verbal.

So my advice regarding public speaking is to never read a speech, but rather to have some palm cards so you can stay on track while you focus on watching the eyes in the audience, making sure that your remarks have been understood, and whether or not the members of the audience agree with them.

My other advice is to self-induce an adrenalin rush just prior to being introduced by the master of ceremonies so you can speak calmly. And also to be aware, as Toastmasters taught when I was much younger, that eighty percent of all we communicate is non-verbal.

Another important thing to understand is that the audience is on your side. The audience wants you to succeed and will be embarrassed if you don't.

The Winds Affect Our Moods

Many years ago, when I was helping coach a junior rugby team when my son was young, I developed the theory that the winds affect our moods.

If you've ever tried to coach a rugby team of young boys on an afternoon with westerly winds, I think you'll understand what I mean.

Actually, I've come to understand that many schoolteachers have the same theory as I do. Also, if I recall correctly, the famous painter Vincent van Gogh cut off one of his ears when the hot winds—called the mistral—had been blowing up from North Africa for about ten days.

And certainly, I know that if you are skiing in good snow on a perfectly still day, your mind goes to a higher level.

How Much Mothers Do for Children

One of my significant learnings from life is how much mothers do for children.

I didn't appreciate, at the time, how much my mother did for my siblings and me. Nor did I understand, at the time, how much my wife did for our children.

Only in later life, now that I've seen how much my daughters have done for my grandchildren, do I realise how much mothers do for children. But I do say to my daughters that they would have had fewer challenges than they did if they'd had a wooden spoon in the kitchen cupboard like my mother did.

Braking When Driving a Car

You may have read about how the brain can be retrained. The following story offers an example from my own life experience.

In my early driving experience, I had only driven cars with a manual gearstick. When I went to do a Master of Engineering degree at Purdue, Indiana, I bought an old Ford V8. It had automatic transmission. It was always easy to start the motor, and it ran well when the engine revs were up a bit, but when only idling it would conk out.

So when the motor was idling, I needed to put my left foot on the brake and push down a little on the accelerator with my right foot. Seeing that there were only two pedals, brake and accelerator, and that I had two feet, it made sense to me to use the right foot for the accelerator and the left foot for the brake.

When I came back to Australia, I got a car with automatic transmission and continued to drive in the same way. I'd normally brake with the left foot, but in an emergency—for example, if a dog ran onto the road—my reflex action would be to brake with the right foot. But somewhere along the line, my reflex braking shifted to my left foot, and has stayed that way ever since.

My brain had been retrained, or had retrained itself.

Mode of Breathing

Another example of the way in which the brain retrains itself involves breathing.

As a child, and through my life until my early thirties, I always breathed in the upper part of my chest. I suffered from asthma in my teenage years and was often tight chested.

When I came to live in Ascot, I started to jog in the morning, before breakfast. I always pushed myself hard at work, so jogging was part of my regime to help me sleep better. Because of knee problems, I jogged on grass on the Ascot State School oval.

As a jogger, I found there were advantages in focusing on breath intake and exhalation. I started to focus on breathing by pushing out my lower abdomen to inhale and contracting it to exhale. This is called diaphragmatic breathing. Somewhere along the line this became my natural way of breathing, without needing to think about it.

Again, I think it is an example of the brain retraining itself.

A Learning from History

I have learned from history that places located along the trade routes prospered. Think of the spice trade. Chinese merchants would bring spices, in their sampans, down and around the southern tip of Malaysia to a port somewhat south of where Kuala

Lumpur is now. The Arab merchants would come across in their dhows, take the spices back to where they could be loaded onto camels, and transport them to somewhere near Beirut. From there, the Venetians would take them by boat up to Venice, and from there they were transported further and sold in countries like France and Germany.

In that era Venice prospered tremendously. Then Vasco de Gama found the sea route from Europe to India, sailing south of the southern tip of Africa. Then the spices started to be taken from the port in Malaysia, down round the Cape of Good Hope and up to Europe.

Venice was significantly impacted economically, until the tourism era of the twentieth century.

So I have learned from that. When I go to a function where canapés and drinks are being served prior to the guests being seated for dinner, I take note of where the waiters and waitresses are emerging from as they move towards the guests. I position myself along those paths, and I do well.

A Learning from the Executive Dining Room

When Main Roads had its headquarters in the building in Spring Hill (now called The Johnson), there was for many years a large cafeteria on floor nine. Off in a corner adjacent to the kitchen was a small executive dining room.

When I gained a promotion to the position of highway planning engineer, I started to attend that dining room for lunch. I didn't know what the criteria were for admission, but nobody ever suggested that I was not welcome or was ineligible.

It was great to have relaxing conversations over lunch, and to hear stories from the past from great characters like Bill Cock and Ken Leitch. If there were any difficult HR issues, these could sometimes be sorted out over lunch.

One thing I could never understand was why all the old guys had a need to get a toothpick at the end of lunch. But I certainly can now. It's called gum recession, or getting long in the tooth.

The Values Drummed into You in Childhood

From my life experience I've come to believe that the values drummed into you as a child stay with you all your life.

When I was a child living down on the farm, my siblings and I were not allowed to leave the kitchen table until everything on our plate was eaten. I find this is true for nearly everyone I know who is of similar age to me. Our parents, as children, had lived through the Great Depression, and waste, to them, was anathema.

I can recall how my mother went about making sponge cakes. She would prepare the cake mixture in a large bowl. Until electric mixers came along, she blended the ingredients by hand. I never knew anyone who could make an eggbeater turn as quickly as she could.

Then she would pour the cake mixture into cake pans that she placed in the oven. Originally it was into the oven of a wood-fired stove, but later an electric oven. She would scrape as much of the cake mixture out of the bowl as she could, using a wooden spoon.

She would then pass the bowl to my siblings and me; we would enjoy the taste of the cake mixture by running our index fingers around the inside of the bowl and then licking them. There was very, very little of the cake mixture that was not consumed in one way or another.

Many years later, when watching cooking shows on television, such as Nigella Lawson, I found it surprising how much food they left in bowls and pans after they had prepared the ingredients and transferred them to other dishes or plates.

Even at this stage of life, I find it very difficult not to eat everything on my plate. That is to say, the values drummed into me as a child have stayed with me all my life.

The Throwaway Society

When I was studying at Purdue University, something that we owned ceased working. I can't recall now what it was, perhaps an alarm clock. I went to a local store and asked where I could take the item to have it repaired.

The response was: why bother getting it repaired when it's cheaper to buy a new one?

That was the moment I first encountered the throwaway society.

A Learning About Modern Electronic Media

In the late 1970s I used to play tennis with three friends. On one occasion we decided to take our families away for a weekend to a resort near Beaudesert, where the children could go horse riding and the men could play tennis.

We drove down on a Friday night. Early on Saturday, after breakfast, the kids went to a horse-riding class.

One of the fathers had just returned from an overseas business trip and had purchased a very early model VHS video camera. He carried it on his shoulder like a TV cameraman, and towed along a two-wheeled trolley that held the battery. He was filming his daughters' horse-riding endeavours.

At one stage, his second daughter was having great difficulty getting up into the saddle. Her foot kept slipping out of the stirrup. I saw it happening and found it slightly amusing. About an hour later the horse riding was over, and our videotaping colleague insisted we all come back to his resort apartment to watch the video he had filmed.

On screen, the endeavours of his daughter to get up into the saddle were absolutely hilarious. It was much, much funnier when viewed on screen than it had been in real life. In reality, it was a tiny event lost to some extent within a wider, active scene. But on the screen it was everything there was to see, and was magnified enormously.

I learned something from that experience. I came to understand how electronic media could take relatively minor issues and magnify them into matters of apparently great significance.

I think this may be the reason why politicians and bureaucrats are now so cautious about making decisions—because modern electronic media can magnify things out of all proportion.

An Earlier Time of Decision and Action

When I look back on my own career, it seems to me that the men in cabinet when I was young were men of action and decision. They were not well educated formally, but they were typically men who had been successful in business—often on the land, in those days—and had held seats on local councils prior to winning seats at state-government level. They had few advisors, and they took advice from the heads of the government departments of which they were minister.

It was a time characterised by decisiveness and action.

A Learning About Myself

When you reach my stage in life, you can look back and see things from a different perspective than you did at the time of events.

I was very good academically, but looking back I can see that I was not an early adopter. I was diligent as a student and had a very good memory. I can still recite 'The Man from Snowy River' right through, off by heart.

I tell people I still have an excellent memory databank, it's just my retrieval mechanism that's not working as well as it once did.

As I said, I was not an early adopter. In my latter years at Main Roads, I used to boast that I was the only person there whose productivity was not impaired if the power went off.

Chapter 11

NEAR MISSES

Rolling a Watermelon Down a Slope

When I was about twelve, my family went for a picnic lunch one weekend to a park on the north side of Brisbane. Also attending the picnic were relatives from my mother's side of the family: her brother and his wife and their three sons, and our maternal grandmother. Our grandmother was small of stature and, at that stage of life, seemed quite frail.

We ate our picnic lunch seated on blankets placed over the grassy area. As we were finishing lunch, my father asked me to go up to our car and bring down the watermelon for dessert. It was a large watermelon, as there were five adults and six children having lunch.

I walked up the hill to the car, which was about twenty-five metres away. When I had the watermelon in my arms, I looked down at the area where our family members were seated.

I saw the back of one of my cousins, who was sitting next to my grandmother. The thought came into my mind that it would be fun to let the watermelon roll down the hill and hit my cousin on the back.

At that stage of my life, I had no concept of momentum.

I released the watermelon. It gained speed as it rolled down the slope and was heading directly for the back of my grandmother. I screamed out, and my uncle, who was sitting opposite my grandmother, jumped to his feet, crouched down directly behind his mother and extended his arms to receive the impact of the watermelon.

When the watermelon struck his arms, it literally exploded into hundreds, if not thousands, of pieces. Fortunately, my uncle's arms were not injured at all, and my grandmother had been saved. If the watermelon had hit her, she would likely have suffered serious injury.

There was no watermelon left for us to eat for dessert. I was chided by my father, and for punishment told to sit in the car by myself for several hours, until the picnic concluded.

Firing an Arrow

Our family used to go on holiday during the August school break. When we were young, we'd go each year to Maroochydore. We spent most of the time fishing.

When I was about thirteen, we had a holiday in northern

New South Wales at a beach just north of Byron Bay. There my brother and I made friends with some local boys who lived on a dairy farm. They had excellent bows and arrows.

There were tree saplings growing in the district that were very springy and made excellent bows. My brother and I brought some home with us.

With some thin cord, we made bows using the saplings. To make arrows, we cut the 'tongues' off some old tongue-and-groove boards using a handsaw. We rounded the edges of the arrow shafts with pieces of broken glass.

Our house on the farm was a Queenslander, set on high stumps, and my brother and I slept in an enclosed side veranda. One day when I was walking below the veranda, my brother had a window open with a gap of about twenty-five millimetres.

He called out, 'I bet you can't hit me.' His eye was visible in the gap.

Normally I would never have fired an arrow at my brother. But as a reflex action to his challenge, I replied without thought, 'I bet you I can.' And I did.

My arrow hit him in the space between his eye and his nose, the spot where you put your index finger if you want to scratch the corner of your eye socket.

How lucky was I that no serious injury occurred. This is an example of why it is so important to think about the consequences before taking action.

For my seventieth birthday, my brother brought to my dinner

party a bow and arrow that he had made for me as a present—and a reminder.

Driving a Tractor into a Barbed-Wire Fence

One day when my brother and I were in our early teens, we helped Dad to spray pesticide on some crops in the back area of our farm. When the work was completed, we gathered up some hare traps that Dad had down at the back paddock.

Dad let me drive the tractor home. He sat on the front of the tractor with his legs forward of the radiator. My brother sat at the rear, where the barrel that held the pesticide was located. The hare traps had been placed there also.

As I was driving adjacent to a barbed-wire fence, one of the hare traps fell off and my brother yelled out. Distracted, I looked back to see what calamity had occurred and ran the front of the tractor directly into one of the wooden posts of the barbed-wire fence.

Fortunately, Dad had not been distracted and had raised his legs in time to avoid any injury. I don't think I got to drive the rest of the way home. But how lucky was I to have not injured Dad.

Driven Through Flood Water

Bob Drew was a classmate of mine at Banyo High School. We both gained Main Roads' scholarships to university. Actually, it was Bob who made me aware of the scholarships.

As Main Roads scholarship holders, we had to work at Main Roads during the university summer holidays. At the end of the third year, we got posted to the Rockhampton District, and spent some time in Emerald and some in Rockhampton.

Whilst at Emerald, we carried out some tasks with a young engineer who was a few years older than us. One day we assisted him in measuring up the quantity of aggregate that contractors had delivered to sites along the Capricorn Highway, in the vicinity of the Drummond Range.

In the mid-afternoon, there was a heavy thunderstorm, with a lot of rain. As we were heading back to Emerald, we came to a creek where the runoff had overtopped the floodway we needed to cross. The depth of water was not great, perhaps four hundred millimetres, but it was running very rapidly.

We waited for some time, but the situation did not improve. We didn't want to have to stay there overnight because we had no food or drinkable water. Our supervisor decided that we should drive through the flooded section.

He said, 'I'll take the cap off the distributor so the motor won't stop if the water is too deep. And I'll get you two guys to hang over the rear wheels of the ute to put more downward pressure on the tyres.'

I was assigned to the tyre on the downstream side of the floodway.

He hit the accelerator and sped into the water. The height of the water on the upstream side of the ute rose up to the level of the door handles, but somehow we got through safely. Being on the downstream side of the vehicle in such rapidly flowing water, I'm sure my life would have been at risk if the ute had been washed off the floodway. I think you will agree that it was a near miss.

Standing on the Running Board

As part of that same holiday experience, for a time I was assigned to a road-construction project south of Rockhampton on the Bruce Highway.

The foreman was Benny Jones. One day I assisted him in collecting some 'witches' hats' (traffic cones) that had been in use during the bitumen-sealing process. He stopped frequently, and I would get out and put the cone in the rear of the ute, then get back in.

The ute had a running board. Down on the farm, I would sometimes stand on the running board of our truck when it was travelling slowly and stopping intermittently, so I decided to do the same and stand on the running board of the ute. Benny Jones had got the vehicle up to a higher speed than our truck, which wouldn't have mattered if he'd braked gradually. But he saw something out of the corner of his eye that he wanted to collect, and he braked suddenly.

I was propelled off the ute. I tried to stay on my feet by sprinting, but my body was travelling faster than my legs could keep up with. As I pitched forward, I rolled my body into a coil, and after several rotations I was back on my feet and still running. I had no significant injuries, just a few bruises. I was lucky I'd played rugby league in high school.

Driving Back to Rockhampton for a Christmas Party

When Bob Drew and I went to Rockhampton district for work experience, we jointly bought a second-hand Holden sedan. As the festive season approached, we decided to drive from Emerald back to Rockhampton to attend a Christmas party our young supervisor had invited us to. Following that, we intended to holiday at Yeppoon.

The Main Roads management in Emerald also wanted us to drive a large utility vehicle to Rockhampton. The ute, which was to be written off, was called a twenty-hundredweight vehicle.

Prior to departure, I had been stationed out at a bridge construction site. I drove a Main Roads ute back to Emerald that morning, expecting Bob to be ready to depart. But he, and some other Main Roads staff, had been partying the night before, and he had concrete test cylinders that needed to be assessed.

So we headed off to Rockhampton in the mid-afternoon, later than I would have preferred. Bob went first, driving our Holden, and I followed in the big old ute. We stopped at Duaringa for a break, and a bit of food and drink. Then we headed off again, this time with me in the lead and Bob following. I think I may have wanted to drive at the maximum speed limit so we were not late for the party.

Between Rockhampton and Duaringa there is a mountain range called the Gogango Range. When the Capricorn Highway was being built through the Gogango Range—or perhaps when it was later upgraded—there was an endeavour to achieve a reasonable design speed.

Coming from Rockhampton, the curves are reasonably good. My understanding is that as the project progressed funds became tight, and consequently the last few curves have a lower design speed. When approaching from the west, those latter curves were the first ones we encountered—after travelling for many kilometres on a straight flat road, and then for several more kilometres on a straight road with a rising gradient.

When I encountered the first tight curve, I was travelling at such a speed that I didn't think I would be able to negotiate it without the vehicle overturning. But I was blessed to be driving a vehicle that was relatively heavy, and with a wide wheelbase. I went around the curve on two wheels, not four. And then continued safely to Rockhampton.

Falling Asleep at the Wheel

Not long after my wife and I had returned to Rockhampton after my period of study at Purdue, we were invited to a Saturday wedding in Toowoomba. We drove down from Rockhampton to Brisbane, where we left our young daughter with my parents, then drove up to Toowoomba. At that time, our daughter was not yet three years old.

On the day after the wedding we drove back to Brisbane to pick up our daughter. We had lunch with my parents, and early that afternoon set off for Rockhampton. Our daughter was in the back seat of the car, in a crib that was not restrained by a seat belt.

My wife and I swapped the role of driver periodically. We'd had a fairly exhausting weekend. On the last exchange of roles, I took the wheel at about the place where the turnoff to Gladstone was located.

It was well after ten pm. I had fought off tiredness and managed to stay alert until we reached the approach to Rockhampton. There was a railway level crossing about three kilometres south of the urban area. When I had crossed the railway line, I must have thought I was safely home. I relaxed and fell asleep, to be woken by the car running off the highway, having strayed across the road into the lane for southbound traffic.

Fortunately, there was no oncoming traffic, and the car had left the road in between the poles that supported the powerlines running parallel to the road, not far from the edge. Even more fortunately, the car had not come to a sudden halt. Our daughter was still asleep in her unrestrained crib on the back seat.

I was able to reverse the car out of the drain beside the road and reach home safely, somewhat before midnight.

The only trouble was that having fought off tiredness for quite some time on that journey, I couldn't get to sleep at all. I must have had too much adrenalin in my bloodstream.

Abseiling with the Road-Reform Team

As I mentioned in the earlier story titled 'Never Read a Speech', I was a member of the road-reform team at Main Roads. If you recall, its purpose was to introduce changes of the sort initiated by Thatcher and Reagan, a shift back to an ideology of free markets, and changes in the roles that government departments played and how they operated.

The project ran from 1988 to 1992. In the initial phase, there was a focus on teambuilding and project planning. The team was taken away for a training/planning session over a few days at a resort in the Tamborine Mountains.

Late one afternoon we were taken to a place where we were shown how to abseil down the face of a small cliff. We were taught how to strap on the gear, and how to control our speed of descent.

As those readers who have done abseiling will know, the cable on which you are descending passes through a device strapped to your body called a carabiner. You lightly hold, in your left hand, the section of cable that is secured at the top of the cliff and passes through the carabiner. With your right hand, you control the angle of the cable on the other side of the carabiner. If the two sections of cable are nearly parallel, your pace of descent is slow. If you move your right hand to increase the angle between the two sections of cable entering and leaving the carabiner, your pace of descent increases.

The next morning, straight after breakfast and without any forewarning, we were taken to the top of a very high cliff with a vertical face. Our challenge was to abseil, one after the other, all the way to the bottom.

The cliff face was so high that we had to change ropes partway down. We were told that at the stopping place there was a twelve-foot ledge where we could stand, and there would be an instructor present to guide and help us shift from one descent cable to the next.

Our team leader said there would be a prize for the person who made the fastest descent.

Several people went ahead of me. Some had all sorts of difficulties, including descending very slowly and getting their legs caught in the indentations in the cliff face.

The person ahead of me became very anxious as his point of departure approached, and he eventually declined to proceed with the descent.

Then it was my turn. Having watched others struggle as they

descended slowly, I decided to give it my best shot and descend rapidly. I moved my right arm well away from the descent cable, and I shot straight down at speed without touching the cliff face.

I heard shouts and screams from above, telling me to stop. I immediately reduced the angle between the sections of rope entering and departing the carabiner, and I pulled up safe and sound at the ledge. My carabiner was very hot.

I had presumed the 'twelve-foot ledge' would be twelve feet wide, that is, jutting out twelve feet from the cliff face. Actually, it was twelve feet long, and only jutted out about one or two feet.

I continued down the second section of the descent and landed safely at the bottom. I knew what a predicament I would have been in if I hadn't been able to reduce my descent speed to zero before reaching the ledge. I was calm, but I suspect the hearts of our team leader and the abseiling instructor were beating rapidly.

That evening, I was the recipient of the prize for the fastest descent.

Chapter 12
SAYINGS

When I was a child living on the family farm, my grandmother had sayings that still stick in my mind:

'If a thing's worth doing, it's worth doing well.'

'If at first you don't succeed, try and try again.'

'If you look after the pennies, the pounds will look after themselves.'

My mother also had a few sayings:

'Always work the willing horse.'

'If you want something done in a hurry, it's quicker to do it yourself.'

'If you don't really need it, it's dear at any price.'

My late mother-in-law had a saying that my wife tells me came from her mother's sister-in-law:

'The only rest is in the grave.'

I have heard various other sayings that have stuck in my mind:

'Genius is saying at the time what you only think of on the way home.'

'There are three great truths in life: your son won't listen to you, but other men's sons will listen to you, and your son will listen to other fathers.'

'You can get almost anything you want in life, if only you know how to ask.'

I once had a recording of a speech given at a graduation ceremony at an American university. It included the saying: 'Value your knees, you'll miss them when they're gone.'

At Main Roads, annual Main Road Old Boys events used to be held close to Christmas in the auditorium on floor ten of the Spring Hill building. In 1988, a lot of older officers had chosen to retire due to a change in the superannuation rules, which made earlier retirement attractive at that time. At the Main Roads Old Boys event that year, I said to John Atkinson: 'John, how are you finding life in retirement?'

'I don't know how I ever had time to go to work,' he replied.

I can certainly empathise with that saying now.

I also have sayings of my own creation, based on my own life experiences. One of them came about as follows.

As I explained in an earlier story, I jogged nearly every morning for fifteen years. Then I walked nearly every morning for ten more years. Then, when my knees could no longer cope with walking, I did aqua-aerobics in my unheated swimming pool each morning for about five years.

The aqua-aerobics involved three different types of kicking. I always had a clock by the pool to count the number of kicks I made in a one-minute or two-minute period, endeavouring to get my pulse rate up. To help pass the time, I would count the number of different types of flowers I could see on the trees and shrubs, some of which were in neighbouring properties.

I came to realise that there were always more flowers existing than I saw at first. Hence, I developed the saying: 'There is more beauty in life than you see at first.'

Another saying that I developed from having a swimming pool: 'Heaven is a place with no trees, if you've been a swimming-pool owner.'

A saying I particularly like is: 'There is a great law of compensation in life.' That is to say, setbacks are balanced by successes. The path to success in life is not all plain sailing. You will encounter setbacks, so you must have persistence and determination.

Another positive saying I like: 'If a door closes, a window opens.'

I once came across a philosophical saying: 'You judge a society by how well it looks after those who can't look after themselves.'

About twelve years ago I had to make an intervention to avoid becoming diabetic. In my annual health check-ups, my blood-glucose levels had been steadily rising, rising. I intervened by changing what I ate. I didn't eat less, but I did eat differently. I gave up all cakes, ice cream, chocolates, biscuits and so on, and even cheese for quite some time.

I never became diabetic. If anyone offered me a piece of cake I would say, 'I'm terribly sorry, but I'm here for a long miserable life, not a short happy one.'

In my life I have taken on the responsibility of organising various events, and this has led me to expressing the following saying frequently: 'Those who just turn up to the event have little idea of all the effort that went into making it happen.'

In my later career, I was a member of the board of management of a major construction project on the Ipswich Motorway. My board colleagues often heard this saying: 'The role of management is to absorb the uncertainty.'

But perhaps the best saying that I have ever heard came from our tour guide, Arman, in Iran. Towards the end of our tour, he said, for reasons I can't recall, 'The past is history, the future's a mystery, but today is a gift.'

When I repeated his words to my sister, she said, 'That's why they call it the "present".'

Chapter 13

PHILOSOPHY

Humans and Planet Earth

If asked my opinion about climate change, or man's impact on planet Earth, or the extinction of species, I answer like this:

'If all this started billions of years ago, out in the galaxy, with a great explosion,

And the energy travelled through space,

And some of the energy turned into matter,

And some of that matter learned how to reproduce itself,

And some of those beings even learned how to contemplate it all,

Then whatever lies behind all of that is hardly going to allow one species to ruin it for all the other species.

Mankind had better watch out.'

A Thought While on the Great Ocean Road

Some years ago, my wife and I spent Christmas and New Year with family members at a beach home on the Mornington Peninsula. We then spent a few days visiting places along the Great Ocean Road. A great job has been done there to provide information for tourists at various stopping points of interest.

On one occasion I stood looking out at the ocean, and at the limestone cliffs along the coastline. I had read about the height of waves that can be experienced there, and about the number of shipwrecks that had occurred. I had read about the limestone cliffs: how the limestone was formed from layers of seashells built up on the seafloor over aeons. And how, in the past, sea levels had fallen when ice ages peaked, and then how, as ice caps melted, the sea ate into the limestone rock layers and formed the limestone cliffs, and the landmarks known as the Twelve Apostles.

I stood there watching the great waves coming in and retreating, coming in and retreating. And I thought to myself: *You know, in the lifespan of this planet, the lifespan of one human is a pretty miniscule thing.*

My Attitude to Work

Looking back, I think that in the first half of my career I would have been viewed as a hard-driving boss. Having grown up on a small-crop family farm, I knew what hard work was. But in the second half of my career, I think my attitude changed. When my children joined the workforce, it made me think about their attitude to work, and whether they were enjoying it.

So, whenever a new employee came to join my area of Main Roads I'd have a chat with them over a cup of tea, at a table in my office, and as they were about to leave I would say in a grave tone: 'But there's one thing I expect from anyone who works here.'

'What's that?' they would reply, with a little tremor in their voice.

'I expect you to enjoy your work. In my philosophy of life, work is the meat of life and pleasure is the dessert. When you go out to a restaurant, of course you want to enjoy the dessert, but why wouldn't you want to enjoy the main course, too?'

And I'd continue. 'I've been working here for many years, and every Monday if I met someone in the lift I would say, "How are you today?" Invariably they would reply, "Not bad for a Monday." And if I saw them again on Thursday and asked, "How are you today?" they would invariably answer, "Not too bad, tomorrow's Friday." What a way to live your life, wishing your life away. I want you to enjoy your work. And if you're not enjoying it, then I want you to come and see me and we'll see what we can do about it.'

I told staff that there were two expressions that were banned from our work areas: 'Not bad for a Monday' and 'Not too bad, tomorrow's Friday.'

I think one of the important factors regarding enjoyment

of work is having the sense that you are making a contribution. Whenever I was to speak at an event, and I was asked to provide a few words that the MC could use in introducing me, I'd ask them to say: 'He has spent his whole career working, as he likes to say, for the good of the people of Queensland.'

On one occasion, however, a very clever young engineer resigned from one of my branches and became a partner in a firm of engineering consultants. When a senior position became vacant, I phoned him and said, 'John, how would you like to come back and work for the good of the people of Queensland?'

'But Kroschie,' he said, 'I'm working for the good of a couple of particular people of Queensland.'

And there's nothing wrong what that.

More About My Attitude to Work

In head-office clerical-support roles, it's perhaps not easy for staff members to feel a sense of contribution to the community. So I would say to a filing clerk: 'Keeping good records is very important to me. If you came to my home, you'd see that I pay great attention to my personal filing records. What you do in your role is very important to me. You might not realise the importance of what you do, but in an organisation like Main Roads we're all little cogs in a big wheel. We're all entitled to take some pride in what Main Roads contributes to the people of Queensland.'

One thing I did hate was 'rework'. When a manager tasks an employee, it is very important that the employee has clarity on what is required and can do it right the first time. I could tolerate one cycle of rework, but beyond that I found the concept very irritating.

I once had a boss who was very clever and very hardworking, but he was a divergent thinker. Every time I performed a task he had given me, he had additional ideas about it that invariably led to me having to do rework, possibly even five or six cycles of rework.

Even More About My Attitude to Work

When I was growing up on the farm, my father said to me, 'Don't follow me, lad, get into something secure.'

Having served my whole career of forty-two and a half years at Main Roads, I guess I followed his advice.

Towards the end of his life, my father, obviously reflecting on his life, said to me, 'How did we do it? How did we make a living growing crops on those small holdings of land?'

'You could do it all again, Dad,' I said. 'But what you wouldn't want to do is go to where I work, and see how much people take home relative to what they produce. You'd have apoplexy.'

In my later career, I was sometimes asked to make a speech to the intake of new graduates. I would include these words in my remarks: 'My generation was loyal to an employer in return for career security, but your generation can't do that. There is so much change and disruption in modern life that you can't be sure that your organisation will continue in its current form and be able to repay your loyalty with a secure job. Your security must come from employability, through skills. You must always be furthering your skills to ensure your employability.'

Looking back, I can see that I was always one to be open and candid, and lay my cards on the table. That was certainly the culture of Main Roads when I joined the organisation. It was a 'doing' organisation, not just a 'regulating' organisation, and was all about getting on with the job.

However, it could be surprising to find, after I had spoken candidly about a matter, that what I said was reported back to someone I never imagined would hear what I said. Looking back, I concede that perhaps some additional tact and diplomacy on my part would have been helpful to my career advancement.

But there is a saying: 'Be true to yourself' or 'To thine own self be true.' That is a perspective that is very well expressed in the poem 'The Guy in the Glass', which I highly recommend to anyone who has not read it.

While attending a course on leadership development years ago, a psychologist said to me: 'Allan, when you were a child in grade one, were you the person the teacher put in charge of the class when they had to leave the room?'

'Yes,' I replied. And I wondered: *How did you know that?*

Perhaps that explains something I would often say to staff

late in my career: 'You mightn't like me, and I couldn't care less, but I'd be very upset if you didn't trust me.'

An Australian Ethos: Help your Neighbour

I once read that Australia was a harsh country for Europeans to settle. In North America, by contrast, people could settle, work hard for a generation and have great success. But in Australia, after a generation of hard work they could lose everything through fire, flood or drought. This caused the development of an ethos in Australia: help your neighbour, because you never know when you will need their help in return.

And isn't that spirit still strongly manifested in Australia today? When we have had major flooding events in Brisbane, it is remarkable to see so many people help their neighbours who have suffered damage clean up the mess.

I'm sure the same spirit was evident in the aftermath of the recent bushfire disasters.

The Pendulum Swings

I have lived long enough to see that, over time, the pendulum swings. As one example, consider the shift to a world of globalisation: an ideology of free markets in a globally open world. It served us well for some decades, but the coronavirus pandemic demonstrated that it is not wise to be totally reliant on another country, especially not for things like medicines and health equipment that might desperately be needed in a crisis. Many countries are in this predicament.

Another thought comes to my mind; the perception that the pendulum needs to swing back.

Some years ago, my wife and I were visiting our daughter and family in London. Our daughter had booked us in to see a performance of *Jerry Springer: The Opera*. At that time I had never heard of Jerry Springer and the kind of television shows he hosted.

The show began with the Jerry Springer character interviewing people on television. They all spoke about their sexual-relationship problems, often using explicit terminology and obscene language. The audience found it amusing.

This went on for quite some time. Just before intermission, someone assassinated Jerry. Then we all went out for refreshments.

When the performance resumed, Jerry had ascended to heaven. Now he was in conversation with God, Jesus and the Virgin Mary. The conversation was focused on the same themes that had dominated the first half of the show, and the same coarse language was used.

And I thought: *This has gone way too far. The pendulum needs to make a big swing back to the standards and values that have helped shape Western civilisation.*

Life is a Strong Force

I have lived in the same home for forty-five years. On occasions over the years I've needed to get rid of feral trees and shrubs that have sprung up in the garden. I would buy some tree poison at the local hardware store and mix it with some turpentine in a small glass jar, about the size of a small cup. I would then cut away a layer of bark on a portion of the stem of the feral tree and paint on the poisonous solution with a small paintbrush. Some days later, the tree would die.

Some years ago, I had a need to do this again, but the poison I bought was of a different type to what I had used previously. A pharmacist told me it would not break down in the soil.

When I applied the poison to a feral shrub, near to a large frangipani tree in my front garden, I inadvertently knocked the little jar over. It did not occur to me to dig up the patch of soil where I spilled the poison and get rid of it. I put some more poison and turps into the little jar and continued the process on other feral trees and plants.

Near the rear of our home there is a large avocado tree. A few metres away used to be a sizeable young palm tree, which I decided to get rid of. I removed some bark and applied the poison liberally.

Some months later, I noticed that the leaves of the frangipani tree had started to fall off prematurely. Another frangipani tree nearby was not yet losing any leaves.

When I realised that my inadvertent spillage had poisoned the frangipani tree, I sought assistance from an arborist, who removed some branches from the frangipani and gave me advice on watering the tree.

Regardless, the tree continued to die back gradually. But so did other trees and shrubs adjacent to the feral ones I had poisoned, where there had been no spillage of poison. Of greatest concern to me was the avocado tree, which started to die back.

Over the next three or four years, the frangipani tree and the avocado tree continued to die back. Small branches of the frangipani tree withered and collapsed. More and more branches on the avocado tree lost all their leaves. I felt certain that both trees were going to die.

Then we had a very dry period in 2019, with hardly any rain. I regularly watered the avocado tree by leaving a hose trickling very slowly so all the water would soak into the ground. There was no noticeable change.

Then we had a lot of rain in early 2020. Both the frangipani tree and the avocado tree are now blossoming with new foliage. They have sprung back to good health.

It makes me think: *Life is a strong force.*

The Stages Men Go Through as They Age

An old gentleman once told me that, as a man, you go through four stages as you age:

>Stage one: You forget the names.
>Stage two: You forget the faces.
>Stage three: You forget to pull your zip up.
>Stage four: You forget to pull your zip down!

I'm only in stage two.

Chapter 14

OTHER LITTLE THINGS THAT HAVE STUCK IN MY MIND

Something Professor McKay Said

At university, when I was studying civil engineering, we had a professor of hydraulics called Gordon McKay. He was of British origin, if I recall correctly. I recall him once saying in a lecture: 'It doesn't matter what we teach you. We could teach you how to make toffee apples, but the important thing is: we teach you how to think.'

Something a Lecturer at Purdue Said

I have another example, this one from my time at the University of Purdue in Indiana, when I was studying for my master's degree in civil engineering. One day a lecturer said, for reasons I cannot now recall: 'The reason why the years seem to pass by more quickly as you age is that one year becomes an increasingly large fraction of the remainder of your life.'

I certainly agree that the time does seem to pass more quickly as you age. I think back to when I was a child, and how long it seemed to take, after Christmas was over, for Santa to come again.

From my own life experience, I have coined the phrase: 'In everything you do in life, the second half seems to go by more quickly than the first half.'

Something Our Headmaster Said at High School

One day on parade at Banyo State High School, our headmaster said: 'Idealism can be very unrewarding.'

Something Said By a Psychologist at a Leadership Course

'We criticise most, in others, that which we most fear in ourselves.'

Something Said About Our Son

I was once dining at the Brisbane Club when I met a man who had once taught our son at Ascot State School. He said to me: 'Your son was the best speller we ever had in grade five at Ascot School.'

I might also mention how we came to name our son Adam. He was our third child, and at the time of his birth, his sisters were aged twelve and nine. I was so delighted when a little boy was born.

The morning after his birth, I was jogging on the Ascot School oval, thinking about names. I thought: *His grandfathers were named Albert and Douglas. His father is Allan. And he is male.* Hence ADAM: *the first man.*

Something Our Eldest Grandson Said

Our daughter and her husband and children were visiting us from London. Their oldest son was only about five or six at the time. One day by the swimming pool, he said to me in his English accent: 'Grandpa, I'm not English, I'm Australianish.'

Negotiations with Our Second London Grandson

On another occasion, when our London family was visiting us, my father was in the full-care nursing home at Hilltop Gardens, where he spent the last year of his life. I invited my two grandsons to come with me to visit their great-grandfather, and they obliged. I thought it was unlikely he would still be alive on their next visit to Australia.

Some days later, I asked them to make a second visit with me. The eldest refused outright. I guess aged-care homes are not greatly attractive to young children. I tried to convince his younger brother to come with me.

His response was the same: 'No.'

During his stay with us, I had noticed that the youngest child loved ice cream, and he loved watermelon. So I said to him: 'If you'll come to visit Great-grandpa, I'll give you an ice cream.'

He shook his head; the meaning was clear: no.

'All right,' I said, 'if you come, I'll give you an ice cream and a watermelon.'

He shook his head again.

'Well,' I said, 'if you'll come, I'll give you two ice creams and a watermelon'.

'No.'

So it continued, with increasing enticements. In the end, for six ice creams and five watermelons, he agreed to come with me to visit his great-grandfather for a final time.

Do you think he might become a great negotiator/businessman?

Something Said By Our Youngest London Grandson

On yet another occasion when the family were visiting us from London, my youngest London grandson and I were sitting by the swimming pool. He was about three.

'Grandpa,' he said, 'you have two names. You're Grandpa, and you're Allan.'

Our neighbours, who had heard his remark, later told me how amusing they thought his observation was.

Message to Our Sydney Grandson on His Tenth Birthday

One of our grandsons lives with his family in Sydney. For many years, I have regularly communicated with him and his younger sister by Skype or Facetime. When he was younger, he was very passionate about mathematics. I would give him exercises to do in arithmetic: addition, subtraction, multiplication and division. I think it is a great shame that educators, with their loathing for rote learning, don't have children learn their multiplication tables by rote as earlier generations did.

For his tenth birthday, I sent my grandson the following message:

Message from Papa on your tenth birthday

You have arrived at a significant milestone on your journey through life. It is the first time that your age will need two digits, not one (a 1 and a 0). You are now a decade old.

Ten is the easiest number to multiply any other number by. I hope that your multiplying becomes easier in the year ahead.

Ten is the basis of the metric system of measurement.

When I was young, length was measured in inches, feet, yards and miles. Now it's measured in millimetres, centimetres, metres and kilometres. (Perhaps I shouldn't have used the term 'milestone' in my opening sentence.)

Weight was measured in ounces, pounds and tons. Now it's measured in milligrams, grams, kilograms and tonnes.

Money was measured in pennies, shillings and pounds. Now it's measured in cents and dollars.

So you can see that ten is the basis of all of our measurement systems today.

So have a very happy tenth birthday, and a wonderful year ahead, and I hope there will come a time when you will need three digits to write your age.

With love

Papa

Message from Our Only Granddaughter

When she was about seven or eight, our only granddaughter sent me the following message by email. It is a treasure. Can you find the missing letter k?

> To my greatest papa
>
> You are the best and i really mean it.
>
> You are one of the best people in the family and the other person is mummy.
>
> I love that you make toys with us and do very nice things with us.
>
> I bet my brother feels the same way as i do. Actually i now.

Letter to a Nephew on His Twenty-first Birthday

As I was completing this book, I remembered a letter I had sent to a nephew on his twenty-first birthday. I think it encapsulates some of the content of this book. The message was as follows:

> I was thinking about what I could get you for your 21st birthday. I thought I'd get you one of the classic success books like *Think and Grow Rich* or *The 7 Habits of Highly Successful People.* And then I thought: Why don't I pen a few things I've learned myself over the years that it would have been good if someone had

told me at 21? (But then I wouldn't have listened to anyone's advice at 21.)

We live in a changing world, with an unfolding future, and success is about positioning yourself to advantage in that unfolding future.

It helps a lot if you know what you want, and if you can work in some calling for which you have a real passion. But success is not just about knowing what you want today; it's also thinking about what you'll need in the future.

Achieving success of any type is a long-term thing, but you'll find there'll be a few opportunities in your life when you can make a lot of money quickly. You'll be too young to benefit from some of them (like the technology bubble of the late 1990s and the recent property boom), and when you're getting old you won't likely be inclined to take the risks to benefit. So you need to keep yourself alert to these emerging opportunities, to have a good source of advice about them, and be willing to take some risks at the right times.

But it is not good enough just to know what to do. Success in life requires more than knowing what to do; it's about doing what you know you should do. You'll meet many people who'll say, 'I could have bought such and such for only so much.' (You might well hear me say it, too.)

'To know, but not to do, is not yet to know.' I think that is the most significant thing I've learned in my life. Or to put it another way, the world pays you for what you do, not for what you know to do but don't get round to.

Success, of course, is about achieving what you want. It doesn't have to be financial. But it probably does mean being the best you can be in your chosen field, or achieving the objectives you set, to the best of your ability.

To do that, you'll probably need the cooperation and support of others. So always behave in ways that earn their trust, and in communications with people, put your focus of attention on them, rather than on your own position and on what you want out of the interaction.

If you have people working for you, always remember: people like to work for people they can trust. And people like leaders they can trust. Tell your people you expect them to enjoy their work. Tell them your philosophy is: Work is the meat of life; pleasure is the dessert. When you go out to dinner, you expect to enjoy the dessert, but why wouldn't you expect to enjoy the main course, too?

The path to success will not be all plain sailing.

You'll encounter setbacks. So you must have persistence and determination.

I've come to believe there is a great law of compensation in life, such that the setbacks are balanced by successes. Some say: 'If a door closes, a window opens.'

Take Grandpa and Grandma Krosch as an example. In 1973, the government took their house and farm and livelihood to build the Brisbane airport project. In the course of time, the Gateway Arterial Road came to be built, close by other land that they owned, and made that land valuable.

There are a number of things you need in your life for happiness. My second daughter once told me of five things you need for happiness. She'd encountered them in something they were learning in acting college. They were:

1. A certain amount of certainty in your life
2. A certain amount of uncertainty (variety, the spice of life, I guess)
3. Love
4. Growth
5. Contribution

I've come to believe that contribution is a very important one; the contribution you make to society and to your fellow human beings. As a leader, one of your roles is to make meaning for your people. Helping them to appreciate that what they do contributes to something bigger, which benefits their fellow human beings, is an important part of that.

But I think the most important thing in life is peace of mind. So always act with integrity.

And you'll find, if you haven't already, that life is easy after a good sleep.

And value your knees; you'll miss them when they're gone.

These are some thoughts that may assist you throughout your life in achieving what you yourself define as success.

Best wishes for your twenty-first and for your life ahead,

Uncle Allan

Conclusion

It is my understanding that stories are very significant with regard to how the mind remembers things. In history, before people were literate they passed on knowledge and values through stories. I understand that was the case with native peoples in various countries.

In the Bible, parables are frequently used. I understand they were a means of communicating concepts in ways that could be readily remembered.

In this book, I have endeavoured to share some stories from my own life experiences, stories based on little things that have stuck in my mind.

I hope you have enjoyed reading them, and that they might have triggered some of the little things that stick in your own mind – which have recalled happy memories for you.

Allan Krosch

www.ingramcontent.com/pod-product-compliance
Lightning Source LLC
Chambersburg PA
CBHW050302010526
44108CB00040B/2091